Countries of the World

Trivia of all countries in the world

Introduction...7

Afghanistan 8

Albania...8

Algeria 8

Andorra 9

Angola 9

Antigua & Barbuda...9

Argentina 10

Armenia 10

Australia..10

Austria 11

Azerbaijan 11

Bahamas 12

Bahrain 12

Bangladesh 12

Barbados 13

Belarus 13

Belgium...14

Belize..14

Benin 14

Bhutan 15

Bolivia...15

Bosnia & Herzegovina 16

Botswana 16

Brazil 17

Brunei 18

Bulgaria 18

Burkina Faso 19

Burundi 19

Cambodia 19

Cameroon...20

Canada 20

Cape Verde 21

Central African Republic 21

Chad...21

Chile 22

China 22

Colombia 23

Comoros...24

Congo 24

Congo Democratic Republic...25

Costa Rica 25

Cote d'Ivoire 26
Croatia 26
Cuba 26
Cyprus 27
Czech Republic 27
Denmark 28
Djibouti 28
Dominica 29
Dominican Republic 29
Ecuador 29
East Timor 30
Egypt 30
El Salvador 30
Equatorial Guinea 31
Eritrea 31
Estonia 31
Ethiopia 32
Fiji 32
Finland 33
France 33
Gabon 34
Gambia 35
Georgia 35
Germany 35
Ghana 36
Greece 36
Grenada 37
Guatemala 37
Guinea 38
Guinea-Bissau 38
Guyana 38
Haiti 38
Honduras 39
Hungary 40
Iceland 40
India 41
Indonesia 42
Iran 43
Iraq 44
Ireland 44
Israel 45
Italy 46

Jamaica 46

Japan 47

Jordan 48

Kazakhstan 48

Kenya 49

Kiribati 49

North Korea 49

South Korea 50

Kosovo 51

Kuwait 51

Kyrgyzstan 51

Laos 52

Latvia 52

Lebanon 52

Lesotho 53

Liberia 53

Libya 53

Liechtenstein 54

Lithuania 55

Luxembourg 55

Macedonia 56

Madagascar 56

Malawi 56

Malaysia 57

Maldives 58

Mali 58

Malta 59

Marshall Islands 59

Mauritania 59

Mauritius 60

Mexico 60

Micronesia 61

Moldova 61

Monaco 61

Mongolia 62

Montenegro 62

Morocco 63

Mozambique 63

Myanmar (Burma) 64

Namibia 64

Nauru 65

Nepal 65

The Netherlands 66
New Zealand 67
Nicaragua 67
Niger 68
Nigeria 68
Norway 69
Oman... 69
Pakistan 70
Palau 71
Palestinian State* 71
Panama 71
Papua New Guinea 72
Paraguay 72
Peru... 72
The Philippines 73
Poland... 74
Portugal 75
Qatar 76
Romania 76
Russia 77
Rwanda 79
St. Kitts & Nevis 79
St. Lucia 79
St. Vincent & The Grenadines.. 79
Samoa 80
San Marino 80
Sao Tome & Principe 81
Saudi Arabia 81
Senegal.. 82
Serbia 82
Seychelles 83
Sierra Leone 83
Singapore.. 84
Slovakia 85
Slovenia 85
Solomon Islands 85
Somalia 85
South Africa 86
South Sudan 86
Spain 87
Sri Lanka 88
Sudan 89

Suriname 89
Swaziland 89
Sweden 90
Switzerland 91
Syria 92
Taiwan 92
Tajikistan 93
Tanzania 93
Thailand 94
Togo 94
Tonga 95
Trinidad & Tobago 95
Tunisia 95
Turkey 95
Turkmenistan 96
Tuvalu 97
Uganda 97
Ukraine 97
United Arab Emirates 98
United Kingdom 99
United States of America 100
Uruguay 101
Uzbekistan 102
Vanuatu 103
Vatican City (Holy See) 103
Venezuela 104
Vietnam 105
Yemen 105
Zambia 106
Zimbabwe 106

Introduction

This is a book about every country in the world; most of the information is fun facts and trivia or just simple information.

This is not an encyclopedia and it includes a variety of facts about each country. Depending on the facts that could be found and are considered interesting, some countries have such a love for football/soccer, which I could not write about Uruguay without writing about the FIFA World Cup in 1950.

The compilation of facts and trivia was made after research, checking and finding what would interest most people.

This is not a useful book about every country in the world, this is intended to be a funny and informative trivia about all countries in the world, which will make you, look a person with so much knowledge that you will impress everyone.

Imagine yourself after reading this book, and saying "Did you know there is an Air Force that has a logo with a flightless bird? **The logo of the Royal New Zealand Air Force is the kiwi, a flightless bird."** This will show everyone how cool you are about knowing such thing, or how nerd you are since you know a logo of the Air Force of a distant country.

This is not only to show knowledge; this is also about the fun of knowing. Did you know that **the most popular TV show in Senegal is a sheep beauty contest, Khar Bii, a reality television show consisting of a search for Senegal's most beautiful ram.** I bet that this is news to you, unless you are into weird things.

Afghanistan

- In 2013 Afghanistan produced more Opium than the rest of the world combined.
- More than fifty years ago, women could pursue a career in medicine or other course and everyday life was very similar to European countries and the USA.
- There is a 65-meter high minaret, the second biggest religious monument of its kind in the world, in the middle of nowhere. (34°24'00.0"N 64°31'00.0"E)
- The border between Afghanistan and China has a 3h30m time lapse, due to the China system of Beijing time.
- It has the lowest literacy rates in the women population, less than 15% of Afghani women can read and write.
- It was the country that received most of the foreign aid in 2012 and 2011.

Albania

- King Zog of Albania was the only national leader in modern times to return fire during an assassination attempt.
- King Zog of Albania also survived 55 assassination attempts
- Albania was the first and only true atheist state. During the communist regime, the religious buildings were transformed in social buildings and clerics were publicly vilified and humiliated, some of them even eliminated.
- Albania was the only country in Europe where Jewish population experienced growth during the Holocaust. However, only 200 Albanian Jews are left in the country today.
- During the communist regime, 700.000 bunkers were built. Today there is 1 bunker for each 4 citizens. They are used by homeless and teens.
- In 2012, more than 50% of the cars in Albania were Mercedes-Benz (Most cars have more than ten years).

Algeria

- Women contribute more to the household income than men.
- The medicine sector is dominated by women, 70% of the lawyers and 60% of the judges are women. 60% of university students are also women.
- In the 1950s, Algeria was the biggest wine exporter, more than France, Spain and Italy combined. In 1961 Algeria was the fourth biggest producer of wine in the world. In 1962 it got its independence and due to French imports restrictions the wine industry of Algeria declined.
- A sand dune on the western edge of the Algerian town of In Salah is advancing on the city and cutting it in half. The dune is moving at a speed of approximately one meter (three feet) every five years.

Andorra

- Andorra has the highest expectancy of life in the world, but only for women, 87.6 years old is the average life expectancy.
- The Co-Prince of Andorra is the President of France and the other Co-Prince is a Spanish bishop, the Urgell bishop.
- All Andorrans should by law, keep a rifle at their home. If not, the Police will loan a rifle to every able bodied man between 21 and 60 in case of emergency.
- Due to a small wayside, WWI technically ended in 1958 as Andorra was forgotten when the Treaty of Versailles was signed.
- In 2009, Andorra had a negative unemployment rate, meaning not only everyone employable in the country had a job, but they also employed foreigners
- Andorra is one of the few countries that does not have an airport, and the nearest is 180km away (112 miles) in Toulouse, France.
- Since 2009, Nigeria is the leading importer of Andorran exports with a share of more than 50% of the Andorran exports.

Angola

- In 2003, a 727 that once flew for American Airlines disappeared in the Luanda Airport, Angola after taking off. It prompted a worldwide search by the FBI and the CIA. The plane has never been found.
- Angola is also the name of a Louisiana State Penitentiary.
- Due to the high grass, Portugal used cavalry units in the Angolan War for independence until 1975.
- Angola also has a ghost town (like Ireland, Spain and China); curiously the town of Kilamba was funded by Chinese companies.
- In 2010 there were approximately 10 million landmines, 1 for 2 inhabitants.
- According to Mercer, Luanda, Angola Capital was the most expensive city for expats in 2014.

Antigua & Barbuda

- Antigua renamed its highest peak in honor of President Obama in 2009, calling it Mount Obama.
- In 2013, Antigua and Barbuda has won a case against the United States at the World Trade Organization (WTO) and is now authorized and moving forward with the granted sanction –*suspension of all American-owned intellectual property rights within the Antigua borders.*
- The largest city has a population of less than 25,000.

Argentina

- During the Argentina's dictatorship, opponents of the regime were drugged, flown out over the Atlantic, and pushed out of planes alive with weights attached to their feet so no bodies would be found as evidence.
- Hundred years ago, in 1914, Argentina was the world's 10th wealthiest nation per capita, the country's income per head was on a par with that of France and Germany, and far ahead of Italy or Spain
- The largest population of Welsh speakers outside of the United Kingdom is in the Chubut Province of Argentina, with 25,000 speakers.
- In 2011, Argentina's government forced McDonald's to sell Big Macs at artificially low prices so that the country's performance would appear better on the Economist's Big Mac Index.

Armenia

- All children aged 6 and up are taught chess at school, as it is a mandatory part of their curriculum.
- In 2011, an old lady in Georgia accidentally cut off the entire internet to neighboring Armenia. She was digging for copper wires to sell and accidently cut off a fiber cable.
- There is a stone structure similar to Stonehenge in Armenia called Karahunj that is actually 3500 years older than Stonehenge itself.
- Armenia is not recognized by only one country, Pakistan. This is mainly due to the Nagorno-Karabakh War.

Australia

- When the Skylab satellite crashed in the town of Esperance, Australia in 1979, Esperance issued NASA a fine of $400 for littering. NASA did not pay the fine.
- In 1970 due to a wheat production quota dispute between a Farming family in west Australia and the Government, the family declared their land to be independent from Australia and created a legal micro nation called the Principality of Hutt River which exists till today, but not recognized by any other country.
- There is a mountain in Australia named Mt. Disappointment, named as the explorers found the view from it subpar and wanted to reflect that.
- There is a Lake Disappointment in Australia. It was named by an explorer who followed creeks to it hoping for a freshwater source, but found a saltwater lake instead.
- A 2012 episode of Peppa Pig was banned from Australia as the central message that spiders were not to be feared was deemed "inappropriate for an Australian audience".

- Australia has 31% of the world's uranium and is one of the biggest sources for uranium in the world.
- During the World War II in Australia, there was a dog whose hearing was so acute that it could warn air force personnel of incoming Japanese planes 20 minutes before they arrived, and before they showed up on radar. "Gunner", a Kelpie, could also differentiate the sounds of allied and enemy aircraft.
- Foster's Lager - the beer brand marketed worldwide as quintessentially Australian - isn't very popular in Australia.
- Last time somebody died from a spider bite in Australia was in 1979
- 'Australia' is derived from the Latin word for 'Southern'.
- When a mountain was found to be taller than Australia's highest mountain, Mount Kosciuszko, their names were swapped so that Mount Kosciuszko remained the highest mountain in Australia.

Austria

- Danish pastries are called 'Bread from Vienna' in Denmark but 'Copenhagen pastries' in Austria.
- 'Austria' is derived from the Latin word for 'Eastern'.
- The town of Fucking, Austria, has had its municipal signs modified to be theft resistant after tourists started stealing them.
- Over 1% of Austria's GDP ($400 billion) is from Red Bull ($4.2 billion)
- *Justizzentrum Leoben* is a prison located in Leoben, Austria, and is considered to be the most luxurious prison in the world.
- Gori, Georgia (the country), birthplace of Josef Stalin, is sister cities with Branau Am Inn, Austria, birthplace of Adolf Hitler.
- The town of Mittelberg in Austria is only accessible by road if you travel through Germany.

Azerbaijan

- There is a form of freestyle rap known as *'meykhana'* that has existed in Azerbaijan since the 1920's.
- The largest KFC in the World is in Baku, Azerbaijan, and it is housed in an old railway station.
- Azerbaijan has a constantly burning mountain fed by natural gas seeping through the surface.
- There is an entirely Jewish village in Azerbaijan, possibly the only completely Jewish town to be found outside of Israel. The town of Red Town (in English) has a population of 3,500.
- The capital of Azerbaijan is Baku and the city is located 92 ft. below sea level making it the lowest lying capital in the world and the largest city in the world below sea level.
- There is a spa in Azerbaijan where you can bathe in petroleum.

Bahamas

- There is an island in the Bahamas inhabited only by swimming pigs.
- Colombian drug trafficker Carlos Lehder bought himself an island in the Bahamas where he put an airstrip which controlled the drugs coming in from South America and entering the US. He became so wealthy he offered to pay Colombia's foreign debt for amnesty.
- The Bahamas were completely uninhabited for 130 years after Spanish conquistadors enslaved, killed, and deported all of the indigenous peoples.
- In 1911 the British government refused to make the Bahamas part of Canada.
- There are 2 different ages of consent in the Bahamas. One for homosexuals (18) and one for heterosexuals (16).
- Only two countries, The Bahamas and The Gambia, should officially be referred to with the article "The".
- From 2006 to 2008, the Royal Bahamas Defense Force's Air Wing had only one plane in service but no trained pilot capable of flying it.

Bahrain

- At one point in 2010, Bahrain had a population of 1,234,567 and only 45% were Bahraini.
- Bahrain World Trade Center is the first skyscraper in the world to integrate wind turbines into its design.
- Bahrain is an island nation.
- Winners of the Bahrain Grand Prix spray Waard (a rosewater drink) instead of Champagne in respect to the country's majority Islamic beliefs.

Bangladesh

- Bangladesh has the higher population density when comparing areas with more than 1 million inhabitants. Dhaka has almost 15 million people in 324 square kilometers, with 44,500 people per squared kilometer. As a comparison, New York City has 10,725 people/km2.
- The border between India and Bangladesh is so complicated; there is a "3rd order enclave": a piece of India within Bangladesh, within India, within Bangladesh.
- The flag of Bangladesh is a red circle with a green background, but the red circle is off-centered so that it'll appear centered when the flag is flying.
- The black soft-shell turtle is a species of turtle that only exists in one man-made pond in Bangladesh. The caretakers do not allow anyone to remove them due to the animals being considered the descendants of sinners who were miraculously turned into turtles.

- In March, 2007, he city of Barisal, hired a circus elephant to demolish illegal properties because they had a shortage of tools and heavy equipment. The elephant was able to pulverize the properties in a matter of minutes.
- Bangladesh has a population of 160 million people and it is the largest country without an Olympic medal.
- Bangladesh was the first country to ban plastic bags in 2001 due to its previous contributions to major flooding.

Barbados

- It is illegal for anyone, even children, to wear camouflage clothing of any kind in Barbados.
- Due to badly designed rules, in a 1994 soccer game, Barbados deliberately scored against them to achieve a draw instead of a one-goal win. Barbados ended winning the game in extra-time by a two-goal margin since goals were valued in double if scored on extra time.
- The current law of Barbados dictates that anyone found engaging in homosexual acts or sodomy can be imprisoned for life.
- Barbados is located east of the Atlantic "Hurricane Alley", meaning unlike other Caribbean islands it is only rarely affected by tropical storms and hurricanes. The last time a hurricane caused any severe damage was 1955.
- A monkey once caused an 8-hour blackout on the entire island of Barbados. It was on Halloween of 2006 the monkey apparently climbed a light pole and tripped an 11,000- and 24,000-volt power line early that morning.
- George Washington only left America for one country, Barbados. George Washington visited Barbados with his brother Lawrence to treat his Tuberculosis. While there, 19 year-old George survived Smallpox, giving him immunity to the disease which later killed so many of his Revolutionary soldiers.

Belarus

- In 2012, after Germany's openly-gay Foreign Minister called the Belarus's President, "Europe's last dictator", he responded that it was "better to be a dictator than gay".
- In 1995, two Americans competing in a European balloon distance race were killed when they accidentally drifted into Belarus, where they were shot down with a missile fired from a helicopter gunship.
- There is a knock off of The Big Bang Theory sitcom in Belarus called The Theorists. Apparently, Warner Brothers cannot sue for copyright infringement because the Belarus Government owns the production company.
- Over 40% of Belarus' entire area is forested.

- According to WHO, Belarus consumes more alcohol per person than any other country in the world with the average person consuming 17.5 liters per year.
- Belarus suffered more radioactive contamination from Chernobyl than Ukraine, home of the nuclear accident.

Belgium

- Belgium has one of the highest divorce rates in the world. In 2010 there were 71 divorces for 100 marriages.
- In 1879 the Belgian postal service tried to use cats to deliver mail. It was unsuccessful.
- In the 1970s, Belgium used to serve children beer at school.
- It was the year of 1955 and a thunderstorm in Belgium set off 40 000 pounds of buried explosives left over from the WW1 battle of Messines. Luckily, the only casualty was a single cow.
- The province Luxembourg in Belgium is nearly twice as big as the actual country Luxembourg.
- Belgium had no federal government for 535 days during 2010-2011, the longest in modern history. Fortunately for Belgians, the local power is so efficient that there were no main problems due to the lack of federal government.
- The word **spa** comes from Spa, Belgium, a city known for its healing mineral springs.
- If your house lies in the middle of the Belgium-Netherlands border, then your sovereignty is determined by the location of your front door.
- In 1990, Belgium's legislature voted to make King Badouin a 'commoner' for several days, with the King's approval, in order to pass an abortion law that he opposed. After the law was enacted, the legislature returned him to the throne.

Belize

- The ruins of a 2,300-year-old Mayan Temple in Belize were destroyed by contractors who wanted to use the bricks for gravel to build a road.
- Belize was the birthplace of chewing gum. Called the "Chicle" in Spanish.
- Belize is the only nation in Central America with English as its official language.
- In Belize, they call speed bumps "Sleeping Policemen".

Benin

- The country with the highest twin birth rate is Benin.
- Benin can be also known as the Central African country of Benin

- The flag of the Benin Empire in Africa used to be a picture of one man decapitating another.

Bhutan

- Bhutan is the only country to have officially adopted the Gross National Happiness index, instead of the gross domestic product, as the main development indicator.
- In Bhutan they have found a very novel use for marijuana: they feed it to pigs because it makes the pigs hungry, which makes them eat more, which makes them fatter thereby resulting in tastier bacon.
- According to the Bhutan legend, Drukpa Kunley (better known as the divine madman) turned demonists into protective deities by hitting them with his penis. Because of this power to subdue demons, Kunley's penis is referred to as the "Thunderbolt of Flaming Wisdom". So in Bhutan, drawing erect penises on things is considered a sign of good luck.
- In 2005, Bhutan became the first country in the world to ban all sales of nicotine products. It is illegal to smoke in Bhutan and citizens may be fined two month's wages. Tourists have to pay a 200% tax on smokes in possession when traveling through customs.
- There are only 8 pilots certified to land at the Paro Airport in Bhutan, nestled in the 16,000 foot peaks of the Himalayas. The airport is a puny 6,500 feet, 2 kilometers long. It may be recommended to take a valium, but you might pass out and miss the view.
- There are parts of Bhutan where there is a practice of courtship ritual called "night hunting" where men sneak into girl's rooms. If they are caught by her father, they will be married.
- Television was only introduced in 1999; Bhutan was the last country on earth to have TV legalized.
- If Bhutanese celebrate birthdays like they do in the west, tens of thousands of them would be cutting cakes and blowing candles on the first day of the year, January 1. Most Bhutanese, excluding the younger generation, are not particular about their birth dates because they do not have exact ones.

Bolivia

- There's a bar in Bolivia called Route 36 that exclusively serves cocaine that's renowned for its purity. Because neighbors constantly complain of noise, and because cocaine is illegal in Bolivia, the bar constantly changes its location which it spreads via word of mouth.
- The San Pedro Prison is a prison in Bolivia where inmates rent their own cells, can live with their families, and charge tourists for tours and at one point produced almost all the cocaine in Bolivia.

- The Salar de Uyuni is a single salt flat, around the size of Jamaica, in Bolivia that contains around half of the world's lithium.
- In 2012, for one day in Bolivia, citizens were not allowed to leave their homes in order to accomplish the first census in 11 years.
- There is no McDonald's in Bolivia: the general population doesn't like fast food, and after years of losses the company finally decided to close the in 2013.
- The primary exporter of Brazil nuts is Bolivia.
- The country has been landlocked since 1879. However it maintains a Navy of 5,000 personnel and dozens of ships which patrol Lake Titicaca and some Bolivian rivers.
- The North Yungas Road, the world's most dangerous road, is in Bolivia where it is mostly no wider than 10ft/3m and has dropoffs of up to 1,830 ft. / 557m, with no guard rails.

Bosnia & Herzegovina

- A Muslim family that saved Jews during the Holocaust was saved by Jews during the genocide in Bosnia.
- A statue of Bruce Lee was placed in Mostar, Bosnia in 2005 because he was something all ethnicities liked and could agree on. It was later vandalized and destroyed.
- Bosnia and Herzegovina has three presidents that rotate every 8 months.
- Bosnia and Herzegovina isn't a landlocked country because of Neum corridor which provides 24.5 km of coastline.
- Vehicle registration plates of Bosnia and Herzegovina were developed in a way that it is not possible to identify the driver's ethnicity (no town, municipality, canton or any entity), all this in order to avoid vandalism.
- The term **Two schools under one roof** refers to the schools in Bosnia and Herzegovina based on the ethnic segregation of children. Children from two ethnic groups, Bosnians and Croats, attend classes in the same building, but physically separated from each other and taught separate curricula. Children from one ethnic group enter the school through one door, while children from other ethnic group through another.

Botswana

- A small portion (14.5%) of Gaborone inhabitants, Botswana's capital, believes HIV is spread through witchcraft.
- Since its independence in 1966, Botswana has enjoyed the highest average economic growth rate in the world, at about 9% a year. It is the least corrupt country in Africa and has a standard of living comparable to Mexico and Turkey.

- Botswana is the plural of Motswana, so a citizen of Botswana is not a Botswanan, but a Motswana.
- Homophobia is illegal in Botswana, even though homosexuality is still illegal in the country.
- Jwaneng mine in Botswana is considered as the world's richest diamond mine producing 12 to 15 million carats per year.
- Pula, the currency of Botswana (a country with up to 70% of its territory covered by desert), means 'rain' in Setswana.

Brazil

- Brazil is the largest producer of coffee in the world, responsible for 34% of the world production of coffee.
- The name Brazil may come from a tree, the *caesalpinia echinata,* also known as Brazilwood or Pau-Brazil.
- Brazil is the world producer of Oranges, accounting for 34% of the world production.
- Brazil prisons offer their prisoners to reduce their sentence for 4 days (up to 48 days/year) for every Book they read and write a report on.
- Brazil was the main destination of slaves during colonialism, only 388,000 slaves were sent to the U.S. one million went to Jamaica and nearly five million went to Brazil.
- Due to the high import taxes for electronics, a single PS4 costs roughly $1850.
- On July 23, 2003, Brazil outlawed the use of tanning beds for minors. The ban was expanded to persons of all ages in 2009. The Brazilian government also deemed the use of tanning beds unnecessary, due to the tropical temperatures in Latin America.
- Brazil has never been on the losing side of a war.
- Brazil has the biggest Japanese community outside of Japan.
- There is a large area over Brazil where the Earth's magnetic field has weakened, it is so large that NASA powers down its satellites when passing over.
- Tiririca, a Brazilian Clown, used slogans including "What does a federal congressman do? I really don't know, but if you vote for me, I'll tell ya" and "It can't get any worse, vote Tiririca". He became the second-most-voted congressman in Brazil's history, with 1,348,295 votes.
- Brazil couldn't afford to send its athletes to Los Angeles for the 1932 Olympics, so they were loaded onto a ship full of coffee and made them sell it on the way.
- The revolution that transformed Brazil into a republic was so uneventful that the few witnesses present didn't even know it happened and the dethroned

Emperor didn't even care. Emperor Pedro II of Brazil did not prevent his overthrow, because he hated being emperor.

- In 1986 a power plug was developed to standardize European sockets. Brazil promptly adopted this plug to increase compatibility with the European market; in the end they were the only ones to adopt it.
- Brazil has an Island so populated with extremely venomous snakes that Humans are banned. Density is as high as one snake per square meter.
- The Brazilians can perform sex change operations for free because it is recognized as a constitutional right.
- São Paulo in Brazil, the fourth largest city in the world, has banned outdoor advertisement. Before banning it, São Paulo was almost covered in ads.

Brunei

- Brunei's government owns an Australian cattle ranch that is larger than the country of Brunei itself.
- President George W. Bush once received a vocabulary-building game from the Sultan of Brunei called "Forgotten English".
- In 2013 Prince Jefri Bolkiah of Brunei blew through 15 billion dollars in personal spending. He bought a yacht that he named Tits and named its tenders Nipple 1 and Nipple 2.
- The Sultan of Brunei lives in the biggest palace in the world; it is four times the size of Versailles.
- The full title of the Sultan of Brunei is *"Kebawah Duli Yang Maha Mulia Paduka Seri Baginda Sultan Haji Hassanal Bolkiah Mu'izzaddin Waddaulah ibni Al-Marhum Sultan Haji Omar 'Ali Saifuddien Sa'adul Khairi Waddien, Sultan dan Yang Di-Pertuan Negara Brunei Darussalam"* the Crown Prince of Brunei's title is 29 words long, and is translated to *"His Royal Highness Heir Apparent Heir Haji Al-eldest lawful son of His Royal Highness Sultan Haji Hassanal Bolkiah Mu'izzaddin Waddaulah"*
- 97% of the exports of Brunei are oil based.

Bulgaria

- During the Serb-Bulgarian war in 1885, Serbia signed a one day armistice in order to allow Red Cross aid convoys to pass through Serbia into Bulgaria, who had no medical corps. Serbia also donated some of their own supplies to Bulgaria.
- In Bulgaria, nodding your head up and down means no, and shaking it from side to side means yes.
- There was a railway bridge built in Bulgaria specifically for the movie "The Expendables 2", after being used for the movie it became part of Bulgaria rail network.

- During the WW2, Bulgaria managed to protect nearly the whole Jewish populace within its borders, even though they were allied with Germany. Boris III of Bulgaria refused to permit the deportation of Bulgarian Jews.
- There is a womb cage in Bulgaria, crafted by humans during Thracian times, that looks exactly like a vagina. During the equinox, a phallus shaped sunbeam fertilizes the uterus altar.
- Bulgaria discontinued the use of the phone number 0888-888-888 because every person who's had it has died prematurely.

Burkina Faso

- Burkina Faso's old coat of arms prominently featured an AK 47.
- Burkina Faso students invented a soap that repels the malaria mosquito, especially important since malaria is the highest cause of death is Sub-Saharan Africa.
- A women's cooperative in Burkina Faso handles all the recycling making its capital the cleanest in Africa, achieving that rank for three years in a row.
- Thomas Sankara, former Burkina Faso president, was one of the first African presidents fighting for women's rights and had an all-women motorcycle personal guard.

Burundi

- From March 2014 to June 2014 it was illegal to jog in Bujumbura, Burundi (East Africa) due to "fears it was being used as a cover for subversion". According to the BBC, Bujumbura residents are known for their "tradition of Saturday morning runs, which started during Burundi's long years of ethnic conflict." The surrounding hills were home to armed militants before 2005 and Bujumbura residents "would try to vent their fear and frustration and claustrophobia, by running, often in a group.
- There is a man-eating crocodile named Gustave still at large in Burundi and is rumored to have killed over 300 people. People have tried to kill/capture him but all attempts have failed.

Cambodia

- Singapore bought billions of cubic feet of sand from Cambodia because Cambodia needed the money and Singapore needed land.
- There are parts of Cambodia where people have made their own trains out of bamboo after regular services stopped running.
- In Cambodia, and also many other southeastern Asian countries, gasoline is sold in 2 liter coke bottles and liquor bottles by small street-side vendors.
- The King of Cambodia is unmarried, has no children, and is a dance instructor. His father once stated that he "loves women as his sisters."

- Angkor Wat in Cambodia is the largest religious structure in the world. It is 80 times bigger than St. Peter's Basilica in the Vatican City, and at least 3.5 times bigger than the Vatican City itself.
- A couple in rural Cambodia terminated their 18-year marriage with a divorce settlement that entailed sawing in two the wooden house they once shared. He did just that.
- In 2011, Cambodia registered a 0% unemployment rate. The reason for the low number of unemployed according to the ILO (The International Labor Organization) is that the majority, over 80%, is employed in the informal sector.

Cameroon

- In 1986 a volcanic lake in Cameroon, Africa burped a CO2 gas cloud that killed 1,746 people in the blink of an eye. 1.6 million tons of CO2 erupted from Lake Nyos in Cameroon, displacing all the air and suffocating the 1,746 people within 25 kilometers of the lake.
- Two men in Cameroon were each sentenced to 5 years in prison for "looking gay", after entering a bar together and ordering Bailey's Irish Cream.
- The capital of Equatorial Guinea is on an island a hundred miles out at sea and closer to Cameroon than the Equatorial Guinea mainland.
- King Ibrahim Njoya of Cameroon had 600 wives and 177 children.
- The Bangwa people in Cameroon traditionally considered friendship so important that many families assigned a best friend to a newborn right along with a spouse.

Canada

- According to a study in 2013, a third of Canadian couples had separate bedrooms in their house.
- The longest street in the world is Yonge Street in Toronto, Canada measuring 1,896 km (1,178 miles).
- During the World War II, prisoners of war in Canada were treated so nicely that they didn't want to leave Canada when released.
- In Canada, no cow can be given artificial hormones to increase its milk production. So no dairy product in Canada contains those hormones.
- At the 1931 World Ice Hockey Championship, the Canadian team was recognized as being so dominant, in such way that they did not participate in the playoff tournament. Canada was put into the gold medal final game, and the tournament was played to determine an opponent. Canada won.
- The tap water in Canada is held to a higher health standard than bottled water.
- The residents of Churchill, Canada leave their cars unlocked to offer an escape for pedestrians who might encounter Polar Bears on Main Street.

- Every year the Netherlands sends 20,000 tulip bulbs to Canada to thank them for their aid in the Second World War.
- There was an experimental program called Mincome in Dauphin, Manitoba during the 1970's that gave everyone a minimum income just for being a citizen. It resulted in slightly fewer hours worked, but saw overall increases in health, happiness, and educational achievement.
- Germany secretly placed a weather station in Canada during the World War 2. It was not discovered until the 70's.
- George Street in St. John's, Newfoundland, has the most bars and pubs per square foot of any street in North America.

Cape Verde
- The Cape Verde islands are part of the same island group as the Canary Islands (part of Spain) and Madeira Islands (part of Portugal), they are known as Macaronesia.
- There is currently no political recognition by the EU of Cape Verde as a European state, but unlike the case of Morocco, there is no formal rejection either.
- The economy of Cape Verde is service-oriented as the most developed economies, with commerce, transport, and public services accounting for more than 70% of GDP

Central African Republic
- The former President, President for Life and then Emperor Jean-Bédel Bokassa of the Central African Republic was alleged to be a cannibal and it is said that he ate the flesh of his political enemies.
- The Colonel Jean-Bedel Bokassa crowned himself Emperor of the Central African Republic in a ceremony that cost 1/4 of his nation's revenue.
- The Emperor Bokassa of the Central African Republic is believed to have or ordered to kill more than 100 children when they protested the uniforms had his image on them.

Chad
- The flags of Chad and Romania are almost indistinguishable and that in 2004 Chad called on the UN to look into the "issue".
- A single small valley in Chad provides over 50% of the nutrient rich dust to the Amazon rain forest.
- There was a war in Chad called the Toyota War, named after the technical the Chadian troops drove to battle.
- Gaddafi tried to annex the central African nation of Chad by getting agents explain to Chadians that they and Libyans were the same people who were only divided by colonialism, while also distributing food and clothing.

Chile

- Chile has a civilian town in Antarctica, complete with a school, hospital, hostel, post office, internet, TV and mobile phone coverage. With 120 people during summer and 80 during winter.
- The September/11 has a different meaning in Chile. It was the date, back in 1973, that the CIA backed the overthrow of a democratic government by Augusto Pinochet, who would go on to kill over 3,000 and torture up to 30,000 Chileans.
- San Alfonso del Mar is a private resort in Algarrobo, Chile and it has the world's largest swimming pool is in Chile. It's over a half mile long (800 meters), contains 66 million gallons of water and cost around $1.75 billion to build.
- There was an experiment in the early 1970s with a centralized computer network that would provide live economic data for "managing resources, detecting problems before they arise, and to experiment with economic policies". It was destroyed when Pinochet's regime took power, before its completion.
- Rain has never been recorded in some parts of the Atacama Desert.
- The most powerful earthquake registered, took place May 22, 1960 in Chile with a magnitude of 9,5

China

- China is a huge country that extends over five different time zones. However since 1949 it has only one time, the Beijing time (UTC/GMT +08:00).
- The Great Wall of China is 6430 kilometers/ 3995 miles long. From New York to Los Angeles, it is only 2776 miles.
- Tree hugging is illegal in China. The law was passed after the mass tree hugging outside of Zhongnanhai a few years ago, the Party concluded that the tree huggers were a dangerous cult and a threat to national unity.
- China is the world leader when producing apples, with a production of 35 million tons, while the USA and European Union combined produce 16 million tons.
- China has the largest population in the world, 19% of the world population.
- China has the largest labor force in the world, with approximately 800 million people available for work.
- Due to its large population, China has 84 cities with more than a million people, more than any other country in the world.
- All pandas in the world are on loan from China, and when a baby Panda is born, by agreement, it is sent back to China to help expand the gene pool.
- The only thing that is keeping China from claiming part of the South China Sea is an old partially-sunken WWII era US warship which the Filipino

government refuses to decommission, thus making it an extension of its government.

- The yellow pencils are related to China, the most common pencils are yellow because, in the 1890's, the world's best pencil graphite came from China. In China, the color yellow is associated with royalty, so American pencil manufacturers started painting their pencils yellow to indicate they contained high-quality Chinese graphite.
- When McDonald's first introduced drive-through to China, the concept was so foreign and people were so curious that many people would pick up their food through the drive-thru, park their cars, and bring the food inside the restaurant to eat it.
- In the 1800's the British actively pushed addictive Opium on the Chinese population to balance a trade deficit. China would only trade silver for their tea and silk and the Brits were going broke. The solution the British found was to sell drugs, and it worked!
- The cost of a tourist visa, in 2013, for China is $130 for Americans and $30 for the rest of the world.
- During China's War of the Three Kingdoms, general Chuko Liang, armed with 100 soldiers, defended a town against Sima Yi's army of 150,000 by ordering his men to hide, throwing open the gates to the town, and sat by the wall strumming a lute. Convinced it was a trap, Yi fled.
- There are some police stations in China that use geese instead of guard dogs to keep watch at night. Geese are very territorial and have better vision than humans.
- In China (and Japan), weak handshakes are preferred as opposed to Anglo countries that prefer firmer handshakes. Gripping too tightly can be considered offensive in some cultures.
- China banned the video game Football Manager because it treated Taiwan and Tibet as separate countries and was deemed "harmful to China's sovereignty and territorial integrity".
- China is the biggest producer of electricity in the world, producing the big number of 5,398,000,000,000 KWH in a year. It is also the biggest consumer, with 5,322,000,000,000 KWH in consumption.

Colombia

- After Pablo Escobar's death, the 4 hippos he kept as pets began to breed and become an invasive species in Colombia.
- There are children in Colombia that need to use a quarter of a mile high zip line above the Rio Negra because it's the only way to get to school.
- The Colombian drug lord Carlos Ledger had so much money, that he offered to pay Colombia's external debt. Not once but twice, and twice rejected.

- In 1921 the United States compensated Colombia with US$25 million and a formal apology from the US Congress for interfering with the separation of Panama from Colombia in 1903.
- The Santa Cruz del Islote is an island off the coast Colombia measuring just .046 square miles, yet it has an astonishing population of 1,200, making it the most densely populated island on earth.
- The cotton-top tamarin is one of the rarest primates in the world with only about 6,000 still living in the wild of Colombia.
- Scientists may have discovered the new "wettest place on Earth". Puerto Lopez has averaged 507.57 inches of rain per year from April 1960 to February 2012. Its wettest year saw 23818.1mm/937.72" (78.14') of rainfall; its driest saw 6195.06mm/243.90" (20.33'), 3x more than the wettest city in the US.

Comoros

- The country of Comoros has changed its flag 6 times in the past 50 years.
- The Mormon Church founder Joseph Smith was obsessed with finding a buried treasure. He may have named the Angel Moroni after Moroni - a town on the Comoros Islands known for pirate treasure.

Congo

- There is a sub culture in Congo of men who dress in brightly colored tailored suits and expensive shoes and who demonstrate impeccable manners and gentlemanly conduct. Some say it is a form of protest and demonstration against the depression caused by the horrors of civil war.
- Congo's president, Mobutu, publicly stated that "It's okay to steal a little", which was consistent with the national mentality that whatever the country had was also yours, as long it is just a little.
- A MMA fighter and UFC veteran visited a Pygmy Tribe in the remote parts of the Congo and filmed local kids touching him as it was "the first time children in the remote parts of Eastern Congo got to see a giant, hairy white man and an iPhone".
- Foreigners should not practice "magic tricks" in the Congo as spirits, magic, and sorcery are all taken very seriously by locals who believe in animism and witchcraft. Many street kids in Congo become homeless because their families thought they were sorcerers.
- The capital of the Rep. of the Congo, Brazzaville, is right next to the capital of the DR Congo, Kinshasa. It is the only place in the world that has two nation's capitals within seeing distance of each other.
- Congo is estimated to have the biggest saving rates of the world, with a gross national saving (personal saving, plus business saving, plus government saving) of 61.4% of their GDP in 2013.

Congo Democratic Republic

- Democratic Republic of the Congo is considered the richest country in the world regarding natural resources even though its citizens are among the poorest.
- In 2010, a plane crashed in the Democratic Republic of Congo, killing 20 people, because everyone onboard ran to one end of the plane and it became severely imbalanced. Why did this happen? They were fleeing a crocodile! Also the croc survived the crash.
- The Democratic Republic of Congo is the world's largest predominantly French speaking country.
- The largest French-speaking city in the world is not Paris (France), but Kinshasa, the capital of the Democratic Republic of the Congo with more than 10 million people.
- The Democratic Republic of the Congo has a city with a larger population than that of any city in the United States, Kinshasa with 10 million people.
- A huge portion of the population, 95%, of the Democratic Republic of Congo lives on $2 a day or less.
- A large percentage of people crossing the border by ferry on the Congo river are blind or are in wheelchairs, as handicapped people get tax breaks on importing goods from Democratic Republic of the Congo.
- The capital of the Rep. of the Congo, Brazzaville, is right next to the capital of the DR Congo, Kinshasa. Only place in the world that has two nation's capitals within seeing distance of each other.

Costa Rica

- Since Costa Rica was not at the Treaty of Versailles, they have been at war with Germany since the WWI, and technically, they are still at war.
- Costa Rica abolished its military and redirected the military budget toward health care, education, and environmental protection over 65 years ago in 1949.
- Until 2012, Costa Rica streets were not named and houses were not numbered. Due to the confusion in the capital, they started naming streets in 2012.
- Nicaraguan troops once accidentally marched into Costa Rica, destroyed a protected forest, dredged the San Juan River, and dumped all the stuff they scooped out of it into Costa Rican territory, all because their commander used Google maps when planning, instead of military charts.
- In 2012 a single Intel's microprocessor factory in Costa Rica was responsible for 5% of the country's GDP and 20% of the exports.
- In 1852 Costa Rica needed a national anthem with which to receive foreign diplomats, so they detained Manuel Gutierrez at gunpoint and threw him in

jail until he composed what is still their national anthem, despite his protests that he knew nothing about musical composition.
- Osa Peninsula in Costa Rica holds approximately 5% of the world's global biodiversity in less than .3% of the world's variable landmass.
- The legal smoking age in Costa Rica is 10 years old.

Cote d'Ivoire

- Cote d'Ivoire is the largest producer of Cocoa, responsible for 35% of the world production of Cocoa. Cocoa is also responsible for around 30% of Cote d'Ivoire exports.
- The largest church in the world is located in Cote d'Ivoire and is nearly an exact replica of the Basilica of St. Peter in Vatican City.
- Drogba, the football/soccer player, pleaded with combatants in Ivory Coast to lay down their arms, resulting in a cease fire after 5 years civil war, he also donated 3 million euros from his Pepsi signing bonus to build a hospital in his home town.
- The nation of Ashanti (modern day Ghana and Ivory Coast) rebelled against British rule because the English governor demanded to sit on a sacred golden stool in a meeting.
- Despite its name, Ivory Coast / Côte d'Ivoire, after a long history of exploitation, war, and poaching, it had an estimated population of only 200-300 elephants in 2011.

Croatia

- In Zagreb there is replication of all 9 planets (at the time) sizes and distances in the same scale as the Sun. In 2004. There was a scavenger hunt to find them because the locations were unknown.
- There is a Sea Organ in Croatia continuously playing music powered by waves that flow through tubes located underneath a set of large marble steps.
- There is a Museum of Broken Relationships in Croatia, exhibiting things like a bottle of breakup tears, a divorced bride's wedding dress, and an axe used to hack an ex's furniture apart.
- Croatia has more than a thousand islands.
- There is a sphinx in Zadar built in the memory of a local's mason wife in 1918.
- Hum is the record holder for the smallest town in the world. It has a population of 17 people.

Cuba

- There are only two countries in the world Coca-Cola is not officially sold, North Korea and Cuba.

- Most people in Cuba still drive old American cars from the 1950's. There are about 60,000 classic American cars in Cuba today even after the embargo was lifted since new cars are still very expensive. The Cuban people could make a fortune off of these "Yank Tanks" since most cars on the road in Cuba are Classic Cars.
- Government vehicles in Cuba are legally required to pick up hitch-hikers if they have room for passengers.
- The US is "leasing" the Guantanamo Bay land from Cuba and writes them annual checks, which they do not recognize and have not cashed for decades.
- Cuba has a literacy rate of almost 100% due to the investment in education.
- Penis enlargement surgeries are free in Cuba.
- Fidel Castro recommended to the Kremlin a harder line against Washington, even suggesting the possibility of nuclear strikes. The pressure stopped after Soviet officials gave Castro a briefing on the ecological impact on Cuba of nuclear strikes on the United States.
- According to the CIA World Factbook, in 2013, Cuba was the country with the biggest tax rate, with taxes over 66% of their GDP.

Cyprus
- There is a 'ghost-town' millionaire resort on the island of Cyprus. The Turkish military does not allow anyone inside and hasn't done so for nearly 40 years.
- After ethnically cleansing Northern Cyprus of Greeks by Turkey, the majority of the population of Northern Cyprus is now made of Turkish settlers and their descendants who have arrived after 1974.
- Cyprus is the only UN-member country that has a map on their flag.

Czech Republic
- There is a Castle in the Czech Republic that has had a 'Bear Moat' filled with actual bears for the past 300 years.
- When Czech Republic conducted their 2011 census, their government discovered that 15,070 Czechs had listed their religious beliefs as "Jedi".
- Czech Republic offers one of the most generous paid parental leave in the world. Czechs may enjoy a 208 weeks/48 months licence.
- There are deer's in the Czech Republic that won't cross into Germany, following the example of parents who learned to avoid the electrified fence there during the Cold War. Even though the electrified fence isn't there for over twenty years.
- Czech Republic had the highest beer consumption per capita for the 18th consecutive year in 2010.
- The Sedlec Ossuary is a Roman Catholic chapel in Czech Republic is decorated with the bones of 40,000-70,000 people.

- The Ministry of Foreign Affairs of the Czech Republic officially recommends the use of "Czechia" as the English one-word name of the country.
- Thieves in the Czech Republic were able to dismantle and steal a 10-ton footbridge (worth millions) by forging paperwork that claimed they were hired to demolish it and to remove the unused railway track underneath to make way for a new cycle route.

Denmark

- On Oct 28, 2013 wind power not only provided 100% of Denmark's power but that at 2:00AM, wind was producing 122% of the country's energy needs.
- In Denmark, it is illegal to burn foreign flags, but not illegal to burn the Danish flag.
- There is a 100% tax on gasoline in Denmark.
- During the WWII, in Denmark, the border guards would screen homecoming Danish by making them say the name of a dessert: *rødgrød med fløde*. Due to its difficulty in pronunciation, German infiltrators could not pass the test.
- In order to get a driving license in Denmark, new drivers must do lessons in traffic related first aid need, driving theory, and have experience in practical driving maneuvers, driving in traffic, and lessons on an advanced slippery track where you learn advanced skid control techniques.
- Bike Helmet Law was defeated in Denmark partly because "the overwhelming evidence is that enforced helmet laws lead to very much less cycling, particularly for utility journeys and amongst young people".
- Due to its unique location, two thirds of Denmark's income used to come from charging people to enter or leave the Baltic Sea, those that refused to pay were sunk.
- In 1946 the United States offered to buy Greenland from Denmark for $100,000,000, Denmark refused.
- The names of the territories of Greenland translate to "much ice", "center", "south" and "darkness".
- Denmark's flag is the oldest flag currently in use, designed in 1219 and unchanged since.

Djibouti

- Russia attempted to colonize a portion of Africa (nowadays Djibouti) during the Scramble for Africa.
- The Bridge of the Horns is a proposed construction project to build a bridge between the coasts of Djibouti and Yemen across the Bab-el-Mandeb, the strait between the Red Sea and Gulf of Aden. It would be constructed by Al Noor Holding Investment to clear submarine and surface vessels, the proposed bridge would have the longest suspension span in the world

measuring 5 km (3.1 mi). The overall length of the entire bridge spanning the Red Sea, starting in Yemen, connecting to the island of Perim, and continuing on to Djibouti on the African continent, would be roughly 28.5 km (17.7 mi). It would have to allow very large ships of the Suez, max size in both directions simultaneously.
- Westboro Baptist Church Hates Djibouti because "[it has] the hottest weather on earth".

Dominica
- There is only one nation in the world that has purple in its national flag; the Flag of Dominica features a purple Sisserou parrot.
- The Boiling Lake in Dominica is 60 meters /200 feet and straight-up boiling 24/7. Reaching a temperature of 197 degrees F (82-91.5 C) on the edges, no one dares to measure the center where it's boiling.
- The Ku Klux Klan attempted to overthrow the Caribbean nation of Dominica by sending 9 heavily armed men there.

Dominican Republic
- The Dominican Republic was one of the very few countries willing to accept mass Jewish immigration during World War II. At the Evian Conference, it offered to accept up to 100,000 Jewish refugees. In 1943, only 645 made it, and each one was given 80 acres of land, 10 cows, a mule, and a horse.
- Tens of thousands of shirts are made for both teams saying they won the Super Bowl. The shirts of the losing team are sent to the Dominican Republic.
- In 1870 the Dominican Republic once voted to join the United States, but the US Senate rejected them. The United States Senate voted to annex the Dominican Republic in 1870. The vote tied 28-28 and failed to proceed.
- Voting is mandatory for all citizens in Dominican Republic, except for the police and armed forces, who aren't allowed to vote at all.
- During his 30 year reign over the Dominican Republic, Rafael Trujillo required churches to post "Trujillo en Tierra, Dios en Cielo," (Trujillo on Earth, God in Heaven).

Ecuador
- Mount Everest may be the tallest mountain in the world, the summit of Chimborazo, is the farthest point from the Earth's center. This is because of the oblate spheroid shape of the planet Earth which is "thicker" around the Equator than measured around the poles.
- The President of Ecuador offered to let the US keep an airbase in his country, but only if Ecuador could have a base in Miami.
- Since 2000, the official currency of Ecuador has been the United States dollar along with 22 other nations.

- Ecuador is the only country to have an embassy for Khalistan and one for Palestine.
- Quito has a very mild climate similar to the UK despite being the closest capital city to the equator; this is due in part to its high elevation.

East Timor
- East Timor declared independence in 1975 from Portugal only to be invaded and occupied by Indonesia later that same year.
- In 1975 Indonesia invaded East Timor, murdering tens of thousands of people, using American "weapons, helicopters, logistical support, food, ammunition." Gerald Ford and Henry Kissinger met with Indonesian leader Suharto the day before the invasion and gave him the green light.
- The coat of arms for East Timor has an AK-47 on it

Egypt
- Bir Tawil is a 2,060 km2 (800 sq. mi) area along the border between Egypt and Sudan, which is claimed by neither country.
- Anwar Sadat of Egypt made peace with Israel in 1979, the first Arab nation to do so. For this, Sadat won the Nobel Peace prize, Egypt was suspended from the Arab League, and Sadat was assassinated.
- In Egypt, actors were not allowed to testify in court because they were seen as professional liars.
- Napoleon Bonaparte's invasion of Egypt in 1798 is a large part why we know so much about Ancient Egypt. He brought a team of 160 scientists, astronomers, engineers, architects, artists, interpreters, and printers to record and document what he found.
- Despite having the most famous Pyramids, Egypt isn't the country with the most pyramids. It is their south neighbor, Sudan and they have approximately 255 pyramids.
- Egypt has been a democracy, but it also was in a "State of Emergency" since 1967 thus bypassing Constitutional rights and democracy until the revolution in 2011.

El Salvador
- In El Salvador abortion is illegal and a woman may be jailed for miscarrying.
- In 26 June 1969, El Salvador won a decisive third football/soccer game 3–2 after extra time. That same day, El Salvador dissolved all diplomatic ties with Honduras, stating that "the government of Honduras has not taken any effective measures to punish these crimes which constitute genocide, nor has it given assurances of indemnification or reparations for the damages caused to Salvadorans". This war is also known as Football War or Soccer War and lasted 4 days.

- MS-13 gang actually started in California and only spread to El Salvador when the U.S. began deporting young Salvadorans by the thousands in 1996.
- A Volcano in El Salvador had been continuously erupting from 1770 to 1958. It was called the "Lighthouse of the Pacific".

Equatorial Guinea

- In 2003 the dictator of Equatorial Guinea took personal control of the national treasury, handing more than $500,000,000 to family members, ostensibly to prevent corruption by civil servants. He has also been declared a god, who "can decide to kill without anyone calling him to account".
- On Christmas, 1979 the first president of Equatorial Guinea had 150 of his opponents killed, soldiers dressed up in Santa Claus outfits and executed them in a football stadium while amplifiers played "Those Were the Days".
- The capital of Equatorial Guinea is on an island a hundred miles out at sea and closer to Cameroon. Oyala, a city in current construction to become the new capital of Equatorial Guinea, and replacing the current capital of Malabo, is projected to have around 200,000 inhabitants and is set to be finished by 2020.
- Despite having a GDP per capita of over $25 000, highest in Africa, over 50% of people in Equatorial Guinea lack access to clean drinking water and 1 in 5 children die before the age of 5.
- Equatorial Guinea is the only African Spanish speaking country.

Eritrea

- Eritrea scores as the country with the least media freedom in the world.
- Sami Cohen is the last Jew in Eritrea, who alone maintains the synagogue and cemetery of the 500-strong community he grew up in.
- In 2011, Eritrea spent 20.9% of GDP on its military, more than any other country in the world.
- During the WWII there was a golf course in Gura that allowed players to lift their golf balls from bomb craters and trenches without penalty, and if a baboon steals a ball, the player can drop another ball no nearer the hole without penalty.
- In Asmara hundreds of millions of USD worth of AFVs tanks have been left to rust over the last three decades.

Estonia

- Estonia has the highest ratio female/male, with 84 women for 100 men.
- It is estimated that 99% of people in Estonia have blue eyes.
- On the longest ice road in Europe, in Estonia, it is illegal to wear a seatbelt, since you might have to make an unexpected and speedy exit from your car.

- The country of Estonia plans to teach all public school students computer programming, starting in grade one.
- Skype was mostly developed in Estonia.
- Estonia declared Internet access a fundamental human right in 2000.
- In Estonia, houses that are located in intersections have two house numbers, one house number for each street.
- Tallinn, in Estonia, is the only European capital with free public transport.

Ethiopia

- Ethiopia donated $5000 to earthquake victims in Mexico because Mexico supported Ethiopia when Italy invaded in 1935.
- There was a famine in Ethiopia from 1983-1985 that killed around 400,000-1,000,000 people and that 56,000 tons of food donated by aid efforts from the West through Live Aid was left to rot in a port by the Ethiopian government.
- Ethiopia was the only African country that was never colonized.
- Dallol, Ethiopia is/was the hottest human settlement on Earth, and is now considered a ghost town.
- Ethiopia adopted Christianity as its state religion in 324 before Rome did in 380.
- Ethiopia is the world's most populous landlocked country with a population over 93,000,000.
- Abebe Bikila of Ethiopia won the 1960 Olympics marathon and set the world record, all this while barefoot.
- The first Italo-Ethiopian War was caused by a language misunderstanding. The Ethiopians believed they were signing a treaty of Friendship while the Italians believe they were being given colonial dominion over Ethiopia.

Fiji

- 53% of people in Fiji have no access to safe drinking water, despite the Fiji Water bottling company's activity there.
- In 2009 after being told they can't publish anything that is negative in nature, relating to the government, The Fiji Daily Post decided to mock the media restrictions handed down by the government by reporting such stories as: "Man gets on bus" and "Breakfast as usual".
- After television was introduced to Fiji in 1995 eating disorders among Fijians skyrocketed.
- There is a tribe in Fiji that grows their bridges with rubber trees.
- There is a resort in Fiji where you can spend the night 40 feet underwater.
- Fiji Population is mainly consisted by the following ethnic groups, Fijian 51%, Indian 44%, European, other Pacific Islanders, Chinese and other 5%.
- There's a tiny heart shaped island in Fiji.

Finland

- The Finnish people are the largest consumer of coffee per capita, 12kg per person in 2008.
- There is a city called Nokia.
- Finland has the most heavy metal bands per capita in the world. While Sweden and Norway have only 27 heavy metal bands per 100,000 inhabitants, Finland boasts double as much, 54 bands per 100,000.
- Finnish babies sleep in cardboard boxes. The government offer expectant mothers a maternity starter kit or a cash grant. 95% opt for the kit which includes a cardboard box that doubles as a crib. It has helped Finland achieve one of the world's lowest infant mortality rates.
- Finland plans to make access to 100 Mbit/s internet a legal right for all citizens by 2015.
- In Finland, speeding fines are calculated as a percentage of the offender's income.
- Finland hosts the Wife Carrying World Championships every year. In which men attempt to carry their wives through an obstacle course the fastest, with the grand prize being his woman's weight in beer.
- Helsinki has a four-times-a-year event called Restaurant Day. The special occasion offers anyone the opportunity to set up a restaurant, café, or bar, for just one day, without having to apply for official permits, as long as alcohol is not on the drinks list.
- There are 2 million saunas in Finland and 99% of Finns take a sauna at least once per week, it is not abnormal for families, acquaintances and even business associates to sauna nude together.
- In Finland (and other Nordic countries) they mostly don't have the restriction of 'trespassing'. You can roam across and camp on nearly all land, pick berries and mushrooms and catch fish.
- The Cocktail Molotov has a starting history in Finland, when Soviet Minister Molotov stated that the cluster bombs being dropped on Finland were actually food, the Finns began sarcastically calling the bombs "Molotov bread baskets," which they responded to with their own "Molotov cocktails", as "a drink to go with the food".
- There is a legal requirement, in Finnish roads, to have your headlights on, whether in summer or winter, in sunlight or darkness, even under the midnight sun.

France

- France is the only country in Europe to be completely self-sufficient in basic food production.

- Child beauty pageants are illegal in France and punishable with up to 2 years in prison.
- The Guillotine was still the official method of execution in France until the death penalty was abolished in 1981. The last guillotining was done on the year of 1977.
- France is the biggest exporter of electricity, exporting 73,000,000,000 KWH, 13% of their production.
- France produces so much nuclear energy that it actually exports energy and makes a profit. France produces 75% of their electricity with nuclear power. In comparison, the US produces 60% more than France, but it accounts for only 19% of US electricity production.
- There is still a part of France in North America, St Pierre & Miquelon; it is only 800 miles northeast of Boston. They have French cars, use the Euro, vote in Frances elections and even have French license plates.
- There is a law in which a bakery has to make all the bread it sells from scratch in order to have the right to be called a bakery.
- There was a woman in France that received a rather substantial phone bill; the total was €11,721,000,000,000,000 (6,000 times the GDP of France itself). The phone company suggested she pay it off in multiple installments and only admitted their error after further pressing. Later, after more calls to the helpline and further wrangling, the company finally admitted it was their mistake and apologized for the distress. Her real bill, €117.21, was also waived.
- Beekeepers in France discovered blue and green honey, the result of bees foraging in the waste created in the production of M&Ms.
- Over the past 800 years, France fought in 185 military battles and won 132 of them, giving the French military the best record of any country in Europe.
- The "Stop" signs in France are in English, but in Quebec, they are in French.
- France is the only country where hamburger sales do not supersede that of other sandwiches, with ham and butter sandwiches (Parisien) being the most popular alternative.
- Approximately 90% of all gunpowder used by the Patriots during the American Revolution was supplied by France.

Gabon

- In 1972, natural nuclear fission reactors were discovered in Gabon, Africa. They operated for a few hundred thousand years and generated an average of 100 kW of power. Oklo is the only place in the world where it was found evidence of long-term natural fission reactions. The fission reaction has been continued, off and on, for hundreds of thousands of years.
- In 1997, logging in Gabon set off a war among Chimpanzees. That "great" war caused the death of four out of five chimps.

- The yellow band on the flag of Gabon represents the Equator, which cuts across the republic.

Gambia

- Only two countries, The Bahamas and The Gambia, should officially be referred to with the article "The".
- The Gambia is the smallest country on the African continent.
- The Gambia regions were divided with names that show the importance of the Gambia River, Banjul, Western, North bank, Lower River, Central River, and Upper River.

Georgia

- Gori, birthplace of Josef Stalin, is sister cities with Branau Am Inn, Austria, birthplace of Adolf Hitler.
- In Georgia there are mountain passes that have been used by invading armies so many times that the farm houses have fortified towers.
- Georgia, the country, is smaller than Georgia, the US state.

Germany

- Germany has the best current account balance, meaning they are the best exporters vs. importers, with a positive balance of $257,100 million.
- The formation of larch trees in the shape of a swastika was discovered in Germany in 1992. The formation, only visible in the fall, went unnoticed for 60 years. After that discovery, other forest swastikas were found in Germany and beyond.
- Fanta was invented during WWII, when Coca-Cola couldn't import syrup into Nazi Germany due to a trade embargo, so instead they invented a new drink, just for Nazi Germany, using only the available ingredients.
- Engineers building a bridge between Germany and Switzerland found that when the two halves met, their elevations differed by 54 cm. Germany bases sea level on the North Sea, and Switzerland by the Mediterranean, someone messed up the correction, doubling it instead of cancelling it out.
- First aid training is required to get a driver's license in Germany in order to ensure that in the event of an accident other drivers will be able to help.
- Each year, 5,000 unexploded bombs from WWII are discovered in Germany.
- Bars in the Veltins-Arena, a major football ground in Gelsenkirchen, are interconnected by a 5-kilometre (3.1 mi) long beer pipeline.
- The name 'Aspirin' was originally a trademark belonging to German pharmaceutical company 'Bayer', but after Germany's loss in WWI the company was forced to hand over the trademark as a part of the Treaty of Versailles in 1919.

- In Germany there are fake bus stops outside many nursing homes to prevent confused senior citizens from wandering off.
- There is a species of deer in Germany who won't cross the border where the Iron Curtain once stood, even though that border has been gone physically for 20 years.
- In Germany, Father's Day is celebrated by groups of males going hiking with one or smaller wagons filled with wine or beer and traditional regional food. Many use this day to get drunk, and alcohol-related traffic accidents multiply by three on this day.
- It is illegal to homeschool in Germany, and homeschooled children may be removed from their parents, even if these children are found to be well taken care of.
- Nazi Germany was the first country in the world to introduce public smoking ban. This happened after German doctors became the first to identify the link between smoking and lung cancer.
- The seal "Made in ..." was created by the British Parliament in 1887 to warn consumers that a product was of poor quality, especially from Germany.

Ghana

- Since Hollywood movie posters cannot be imported to Ghana, locals will try their hand at drawing them.
- In 2013 a Chinese company sold over 110 million counterfeit condoms to Ghana.
- In January 1997, the capital of Ghana rioted over accusations of penis snatching wizards. Several people were killed by mobs who accused them of using magic handshakes to kidnap penises and hold them for ransom.
- In Ghana it is desirable to be buried in a novelty coffin, with favorite items including a huge Coke bottle, an oversized Nokia and a giant catfish.
- Ghana is undertaking a $10 billion technology park project that will feature six towers, one of which will be the tallest in Africa. It is called H.O.P.E., Home, Office, People and Environment.
- In 1983, Nigeria lead a campaign to expel 2 million Ghanaian immigrants after they were scapegoated for Nigeria's social and economic woes after the oil boom started to wane. This movement was known as "Ghana Must go".
- In Ghana, sex between two men is illegal but sex between two women is legal.

Greece

- There was a Greek prime minister in 1830's that tried to spread the potato in Greece, but people were not interested, so he made a wise choice, he put armed guards in front of shipments of potatoes so people would think they were important. Later, people started stealing these potatoes which spread the crop to all of Greece.

- In 2012, 11% of Greece's homeless had a university degree.
- During WW2, Italy delivered an ultimatum to Greece demanding they accept occupation. The Greeks replied with "Then it is war". In the ensuing fight, the outgunned Greeks put Italy on the defensive, forcing Germany to intervene, diverting resources from the upcoming invasion of the USSR.
- Chios has, each year, a 'fireworks war' is held by two nearby towns, where the objective is to hit each other's town bell.
- Greece is officially known as the Hellenic Republic.
- Mount Athos is an autonomous region in Greece that has forbid the entry of women for 1,000 years. In the 14th Century a Greek king's wife was brought to the area to avoid the plague, but she was carried by hand-carriage the entire time to avoid touching the ground.
- The oldest olive tree can be found in Chania. Its age is estimated to be around 4,000 years old and still produces olive oil as of today
- The 26.2 mile / 42 kilometers length of a marathon was not established in Ancient Greece, but in 20th Century London as the length between Windsor Castle and the Olympic Stadium. Before this, marathon distances were arbitrary and varied by several miles.

Grenada

- Grenada celebrates Thanksgiving in 25th October to commemorate the US invasion in 1983.
- There is an underwater volcano named "Kick 'em Jenny" north of the island of Grenada
- The little symbol on the flag of Grenada is a raw nutmeg.
- Sauteurs is French for "Jumpers". It was named for the last Caribe people on the island who committed suicide by jumping from a cliff rather than face domination by the French.

Guatemala

- The United Fruit Company's (UFC now known as Chiquita) main rival was Guatemala, who exported lots of fruit. To eliminate them, UFC lied to the US government that Guatemala's government was Pro-Soviet. The US staged a coup, which led to the 36 year long Guatemalan civil war.
- In 2013, Guatemala had the highest death rate from violence in the world, at 74.9 deaths per 100,000 population.
- The president of Guatemala from 1898-1920 (Manuel Estrada Cabrera), tried to establish a cult of Minerva in Guatemala, and built Greek style temples around Guatemala dedicated to her.

- Guatemala Special Forces (Kaibiles) trainees will raise and bond with a puppy before killing it and eating it.

Guinea

- When Guinea declared its independence from France, the French reacted by burning files, cutting telephone lines, and even ripped electrical sockets out of walls before leaving the country, effectively cutting off all aid.
- The origin of the Ebola epidemic in West Africa was traced to a 2 year old child who died on December 6, 2013, in the village of Méliandou in southern Guinea. The child may have contracted Ebola from eating fruit contaminated by a fruit bat.

Guinea-Bissau

- Only 14% of the population of Guinea Bissau speaks the official language, Portuguese.

Guyana

- Indians are the largest ethnic group, the descendants of indentured laborers from India, who make up about 43.5% of the population of Guyana.
- When thousands of East Indians immigrated to the South American country of Guyana in the 19th century, the Brahmins abolished all caste-distinguishing practices to fight off conversion attempts by Christian missionaries. The country is composed by nearly 30% Hinduism people.
- Janet Jagan was the first female president of Guyana; she was also the first US-born and Jewish leader of that nation.

Haiti

- Haiti was founded after a slave rebellion against the French. Inspired by the French Revolution of 1789 and principles of the rights of man, free people of color and slaves in Saint-Domingue and the French West Indies pressed for freedom and more civil rights. The most important revolution was the one of the slaves in Saint-Domingue, starting in the northern plains in 1791, where Africans greatly outnumbered the whites.
- Until 1936, Liechtenstein and Haiti were unknowingly using the same flag, and they didn't find out until they competed against each other in the Olympics.
- After achieving independence from France, Haiti was forced to pay 150 million francs (later reduced to 60 million) in reparations to the French slaveholders in order for France to recognize their sovereignty. The payments started in 1825 and the last payment was made in 1947.
- Haitian government got less than 1% of the money given after the earthquake. Haiti is often called the "Republic of NGOs".

- Haiti's land was 60% forest coverage in 1923. Now because of deforestation it's down to 2%.
- François Duvalier, former president of Haiti, despite a prohibition against presidential reelection, ran for office and won with an official tally of 1,320,748 votes to 0.
- In 1963, Papa Doc, the former dictator of Haiti, was once convinced that a principal enemy had transformed himself into a black dog, so he ordered all black dogs in the nation to be killed.
- The US did not recognize the independence of Haiti (the second in the western hemisphere) because President Jefferson feared a slave revolt at home, and in fact imposed a trade embargo.
- The US invaded Haiti in 1915 and retained complete economic control of the island nation until 1934. This was done to support the interests of a sugar company and to break local laws that forbid foreign ownership of property.

Honduras

- The murder rate in Honduras is so high that some cities have had to start offering a program for free funerals. There is a violent death in Honduras every 74 minute.
- A factory in Honduras got famous in the news after forcing its workers to wear diapers for the sake of efficiency.
- In the 26 of June 1969, Honduras lost a decisive third game 3-2 after extra time. That same day, El Salvador dissolved all diplomatic ties with Honduras, stating that "the government of Honduras has not taken any effective measures to punish these crimes which constitute genocide, nor has it given assurances of indemnification or reparations for the damages caused to Salvadorans. This war is also known as Football War or Soccer War and lasted 4 days
- Almost every year from the mid 1800's to present day, Yoro has a storm that rains actual fish.
- In 1937, Nicaragua and Honduras almost came to a state of war over a stamp. In August of that year, the Nicaraguan postal service released a new set of Airmail stamps, centered on a map of Nicaragua. The map also showed part of Honduras, north of the border, in the same shading as Nicaragua proper. Although the accepted border between both countries was also shown, the part of Honduras shaded as Nicaragua was labeled Territorio en Litigio ('Territory in Dispute').
- It is illegal to carry a passenger on your motorcycle in Honduras because of drive-by-shootings.
- In 1998, Hurricane Mitch destroyed 80% of Honduras' roads, 33,000 homes, 70% of its planted crops, setting the country back 50 years.

- Banana republic came from the humorist O. Henry coining the term "Banana Republic" in 1904 to refer to the notorious Chiquita and its actions in Honduras.

Hungary

- The Hungarian name for Hungary is Magyarország.
- In Hungary, as other European and northern countries, you're legally allowed to name your child from a pre-approved list of names. If you want to name them something else you need to submit an application.
- There was a bridge in southern Hungary that was found to still be rigged with dynamite from World War II, all this in October of 1999, 54 years after the end of the war.
- After the First World War, Hungary (Part of Austro-Hungary Empire) lost 72% off his territory.
- In the United States and Hungary, the phrase "The devil is beating his wife" can be used to mean the sun is shining while it is raining out.
- Zwack is a Hungarian company that makes among other liqueurs and spirits, an 80 proof (40% alcohol), herbal liqueur known as Unicum with a secret blend of more than forty different herbs and spices. It is known as the National Shot of Hungary.
- Hungary national football team only had one defeat between 1950 and 1956, and that was the World Cup final.
- Hungarians use family names before given names and Hungary is the only Western country to do so.
- An animal as the sheep-pig exists. It is known as the Mangalitsa, the animal was first bred in Hungary during the nineteenth century to produce more lard-laced meat. Resulting in a pig with the body of a porker and the curly-haired coat of a sheep. Often considered a delicacy by chefs who prefer higher fat content.
- King Béla I of Hungary died when his throne collapsed underneath him.
- In July 1946, Hungary experienced the worst inflation ever recorded with an inflation rate of 41,900,000,000,000,000%. The banknote with the largest denomination was 100,000,000,000,000,000,000 (100 Quintillion) pengő, which was equal to about US$0.20. Some days, the prices doubled every 15 hours.

Iceland

- A 1999 law sets, everyone in Iceland pays church tax, and the payment of those unaffiliated with a church goes to the University of Iceland.
- Only one person has been killed by armed police in Iceland since it became an independent republic in 1944.

- Iceland has no army and is also recognized as the world's most peaceful country. Since Iceland does not have an Air Force it relies on its allies to provide protection.
- Iceland is so small that virtually everyone is related but big enough so that you don't know how you're related.
- The traditional naming customs of Iceland differ in a way that they follow no family lineage. Men are named after their father. I.e. If Jon has a son named Olaf, his name is Olaf Jonsson. If Olaf then has a son named Magnus, his name is Magnus Olafsson. Women are similar with the suffix 'dottir'. If the children were born to Icelandic women and American or British servicemen, they were often given the last name Hansson meaning "his son" as their fathers were either unknown or had left Iceland.
- Iceland's electricity is produced entirely from renewable energy sources (hydroelectric 70% and geothermal 30%).
- Volcanic activity provides Reykjavík with geothermal heating systems for both residential and industrial districts. In 2008, natural hot water was used to heat roughly 90% of all buildings in Iceland.
- The only police officers that carry guns in Iceland are part of the elite "Viking Squad".
- In 1783 when the volcanic fissure Laki erupted, the fallout in Iceland caused around 80% of sheep, 50% of cattle and 50% of horses to die as well as killing an estimated 20–25% of the country's human population while also creating worldwide effects.
- Iceland has one big circle of road ("Ring Road") that connects all habitable parts of the country.

India

- India is home to over 250 million cows.
- The border between India and Bangladesh is so complicated; there is a "3rd order enclave": a piece of India within Bangladesh, within India, within Bangladesh.
- Jews arrived in India 2500 years ago and unlike many parts of the world, Jews lived in India without any instances of anti-Semitism from the local majority populace until the Portuguese and British started the colonization of India.
- The Lotus Temple is a golden temple in India that feeds thousands of people who show up randomly regardless of race, religion and class.
- Sex toys are illegal in India, and their sale punishable by 2 years in prison.
- There is a tribe in India that has passed down for generations the art of manipulating tree roots to create a system of "living" bridges.
- India has 814 million registered voters, 900,000 polling stations and it takes 9 days to vote for the government. Indian Voters also get to record their

displeasure with all the candidates, with the introduction of the "none of the above" option on the ballot.

- In 1954, the city of Bombay, India had such a bad rat problem that they began accepting dead rats in place of taxes. This led to the mass breeding and killing of rats to use them for payment.
- When the English colonial government in Delhi put a bounty on cobras to eliminate them from the city, it resulted in a cobra population boom. The bounty was greater than the cost of breeding a cobra, and the citizens were breeding them to sell to the government.
- Nehru rejected permanent membership for India on the UN Security Council to keep India out of Cold War politics.
- In 2013, 5% of India's population was on Facebook, but it already had the third largest Facebook population in the world.
- In Bangalore, the government shames property tax defaulters by sending drummers to make noise and wave banners outside of their properties until they pay their taxes.
- In order to promote lower birth rates, authorities have created a sterilization lottery. Individuals that volunteer to be sterilized are given 600 rupees and their names are put into a lottery to win televisions, motorcycles, food processors, and the grand prize, a Tata Nano.
- In order to prevent female infanticide, it is illegal to know the sex of the baby before birth.
- With 150,000 post offices, India has the largest postal network in the world. However, it is not unusual for a letter to take two weeks to travel just 30 miles.
- In India, the definition of rape includes "men who lead women to believe they will marry them, and then fail to follow through with it".
- The Election Commission of India stipulates that no person should have to travel more than 2 kilometers to cast a vote. So in the state of Gujarat, a temple caretaker who lives in an ancient deserted temple gets his own special voting booth, just for him to vote.

Indonesia

- Upon entering Indonesia, you are greeted with a sign that threatens death to drug traffickers.
- The $100 billion tobacco industry in Indonesia is virtually unregulated. With grade school aged children as a prime target, it is common for males to start smoking as early as age 6. Tobacco smoke is also used as a holistic treatment for diseases and cancers of the body.
- Indonesia is the largest Muslim country in the world by population.

- Indonesia, the world's most populous Muslim nation, recognizes the right to practice six religions in total: Islam, Protestant, Catholic, Hindu, Buddhism and Confucianism. Atheism is illegal.
- It is common practice in Indonesia for the hospital to keep newborn babies until the bill is paid.
- In Indonesia (and some other countries) it is not uncommon for people to only have one name (i.e. a given first name). However, when they immigrate to the United States, their given name becomes their last name and their first name legally becomes 'FNU' which stands for 'First Name Unknown'.
- The Lakes of Mount Kelimutu of Indonesia can change color from blue to green to black or red unpredictably.
- Indonesia shares its flag colors and shape with Monaco.
- The 1815 eruption of Mount Tambora in Indonesia resulted in severe climate abnormalities in 1816, nicknamed the "Year without a summer".
- Garuda (the symbol of Indonesia) has 17 wing feathers, 8 on the lower tail, 19 on the upper tail and 45 on the neck. Together, this makes 17 august 1945, the date of Indonesia's Independence.
- The island of Java in Indonesia has a population roughly equal to Russia, despite being over 120 times smaller.

Iran

- Iran once arrested 14 squirrels for spying
- 70% of Iran's science and engineering students are women.
- There is a massive rain forest in the north of Iran, a country in a region of deserts.
- Iran only classes three organizations as terrorist groups, and two of them are the CIA and the American Army.
- Iran is the only country where mandatory contraceptive courses are required for both males and females before a marriage license can be obtained.
- In 1953, Iran had a democratically elected prime minister. The US and the UK violently overthrew him, and installed a west friendly monarch in order to give British Petroleum, then AIOC, unrestricted access to the country's resources.
- In July 2010, the Islamic government of Iran issued updated grooming guidelines to men. Among the new regulations is a ban of the mullet hairstyle.
- Iran is home to the largest population of Jews in the Middle East, outside Israel.
- Iran currently is the only country in the world that allows the sale of one's kidney for compensation; consequently, the country does not have either a waiting list or a shortage of available organs.

- There is a place in Iran known as the Valley of Genitalia, where statues representing female breasts and male genitals date from 1000 AD to 70 years ago.
- "Iran" means "Land of the Aryans".
- Homosexuality in Iran is punishable by death, however transsexualism is legal and the government even pays for sex changes. They carry out more sex change operations than any other nation in the world except for Thailand, and recognize sex changes on birth certificates.

Iraq

- A natural gas vent in Iraq known as The Eternal Fire has been burning continuously for over 4,000 years, and is mentioned by Herodotus, Plutarch, and in the Old Testament's Book of Daniel.
- Iraq has a similar system to universal health care, provided by funding from the US.
- A man built a restaurant in Northern Iraq called MaDonal's after McDonald's turned denied his request. The restaurant serves items such as "Big Macks," and serves free food to U.S. forces, and thus has been threatened by suicide bombers, turning the man into a local celebrity.
- In 2002 Iraq's Vice President suggested a duel between George W. Bush and Saddam Hussein, to be refereed by Kofi Annan, as a way to settle their disputes without going to war.
- The largest Embassy in the world is the U.S. Embassy in Iraq. It cost $750 million to build, employs 16,000 people and costs $6 billion a year to run.

Ireland

- Murderers in medieval Ireland were given to the deceased's family as slaves, if they failed to pay a hefty fine to buy their freedom. The family could then legally kill the murderer themselves.
- It was a tradition in Ireland that if you donated a pint of blood, they'd give you a pint of Guinness to replace the iron. However this was cancelled in 2012.
- At the height of the Irish Potato Famine in 1847, almost 4,000 ships carried food from Ireland to England and Scotland while 400,000 Irish died of starvation and related diseases. The same year, a Native American tribe sent an estimated value of $710 to help ease the suffering.
- Ireland has never recovered its population numbers from before The Great Famine (potato famine). It was over 8 million in 1845, and only about 5 million today.
- Ireland is the only country in the world with a musical instrument as its symbol.

- Before 1939 in Ireland, if a Guinness brewer wished to marry a Catholic, his resignation was requested.
- In 2010 an unlucky airline passenger was arrested in Ireland after Slovak security officials placed explosives in his luggage for training, and then forgot to remove them before the plane took off.
- Whiskey is unique from Ireland. Whiskey with an "e" comes from Ireland whilst Whisky without an "e" comes from Scotland and Canada.
- There is a town in Ireland that hosts a fair in which a goat is crowned king for 3 days and hoisted on a 40 foot / 12 meters pedestal.
- In Ireland the police were looking for a Polish man called Mr. Prawo Jazdy for over 50 driving offences across the country, they later found out prawo jazdy means driving license in polish.
- Happy Hour is illegal in Ireland since 2003
- Two-thirds of the barley produced in Ireland is used for brewing Guinness.

Israel

- In 1965, seeds that were dated to 2,000 years old were discovered in an ancient jar in Israel. The seeds were kept in storage for 40 years and after they were planted, a tree that had been extinct for over 1800 years sprouted.
- Women were allowed to enter combat roles in the Israel. They performed at a level equal to men but the program was still abolished for two reasons: Islamist fighters refused to surrender to women, and the men in the unit would lose all combat discipline when a woman was injured.
- In 1952 Albert Einstein was offered the Presidency of the State of Israel. He declined, saying that as a scientist trained to deal with objective facts, he lacked the aptitude and experience to deal with people.
- Immediately after the founding of Israel on May 14, 1948, before their defense force was even founded, five Arab nations (Egypt, Iraq, Syria, Lebanon, and Jordan) declared war on it.
- Publications in Israel have to disclose whether a fashion model was made to look thinner through photo manipulation.
- In Israel, on Yom Kippur eve, so much of the population is observing the holiday that the streets are almost completely empty, and secular Israelis have made it a holiday tradition to bike and rollerblade through the empty streets.
- Israel is the only country in the world with a mandatory military service requirement for women. They comprise 51% of all officers.
- There is a city in Israel called "Oasis of Peace", where Jews and Muslims are raised and educated together.

- Israel produces 35% of its fresh water from desalination plants, enough that they have a surplus and aims to have 70% of their fresh water supplied from desalination by 2050.

Italy

- Tomatoes are originally from the American continent and were not introduced in Italy until the 1540s.
- The fork came to Italy before any other European country because of pasta.
- Beretta is the oldest gun company in the world being established in 1526 in Brescia.
- The 'peperoni' is the Italian word for 'bell pepper' and if you order a 'peperoni pizza' in Italy, you will get a pizza with sliced bell peppers on it.
- Since the Vatican is so tiny, all embassies to it are actually located in Italy. This includes Italy's embassy to the Vatican, which is the only embassy in the world on its own nation's soil.
- When modern Italy was formed, the Florentine dialect was chosen as the universal language largely due to the works of Dante.
- In 2011, Italy became the first country in Europe to ban non-biodegradable plastic bags.
- Italy has a 13 foot tall sculpture of a middle finger in front of their stock exchange.
- Pittsburgh, Pennsylvania, with its three rivers, is the city with the most bridges in the world, three more than former world leader Venice, Italy.
- Craco is a mostly intact medieval village in Italy that has been abandoned and now serves as a destination for filmmakers and the occasional tourist.
- Italy is the leading producer of the Kiwi in the world, despite having origins in Southern China.
- Italian national sports teams wear Blue (instead of their flag colors of Green, White, and Red) to honor the House of Savoy, under whom Italy was unified in 1861.

Jamaica

- In Jamaica sex between men is punishable with up to ten years imprisonment. Sex between women has no problem at all.
- In 2008 a beach was stolen in Jamaica. The 500 truckloads of sand remain missing to this very day.
- Irish people are the second largest ethnic group in Jamaica after African. Irish Jamaicans constitute up to 25% of Jamaica's population.
- Jamaica has been described by human-rights groups as the most homophobic place on earth. Men are even afraid to seek treatment for HIV out of fear they will be associated with homosexuals.

- Jamaica has the lowest combined rate of drug and alcohol related deaths in the World.
- There are more Jamaicans living outside Jamaica, than there is on the island.
- In 1700 the Jamaican population consisted of 7,000 English to every 40,000 African slaves.

Japan

- Japan is home of the largest urban area in the world, the Tokyo-Yokohama area has more than 37 million people.
- Japan has the highest expectancy of life in the world, with 84.6 years old as the average life expectancy of Japanese.
- Japan has the highest public debt in the world, 226% of their GDP, meaning they would have to work 825 days only to pay off their debt.
- In 1912, Japan sent the USA some Japanese Cherry Trees as a sign of their blossoming friendship. After WW2, Japan's Cherry Trees were weak and sick so the USA sent a bunch of them back to reinvigorate their trees.
- The oldest company in the world is Kongō Gumi, a construction company in Japan, which has been around since the year 578 AD.
- Sleeping on the job is acceptable in Japan. It is viewed as exhaustion from working hard. Some people fake it to look committed to their job.
- Due to the specific Japanese culture, the only Japanese who survived the Titanic lost his job because he was known as a coward in Japan for not dying with the other passengers.
- In Japan, prisoners on death row are not told when they will be executed until a few hours before they are hanged, and their families are not notified until after they are dead.
- There have been over 200 flavors of Kit-Kat in Japan.
- In Japan gambling is illegal; the way they get around the law is to give out prizes instead of cash, which the winner can then sell back to the establishment for cash.
- Any "Kobe" beef purchased outside of Japan or China is fake, since actual Kobe beef must be raised in specific parts of Japan, and is illegal to export anywhere other than China.
- In feudal Japan, merchants were the lowest class because unlike farmers and artisans, they don't actually produce anything.
- There is a pepper grown in Japan called the Shishito pepper, only 1 out of 10 is spicy and there's no way of knowing beforehand.
- Macaques monkeys in Japan learned to steal purses and wallets, and take out the coins use them to buy drinks and snacks from vending machines.
- Yasuke, a 16th century African who traveled to Japan as a slave, caused such a sensation that a powerful warlord wished to see him. He thought his black

skin was paint and ordered it to be scrubbed. However, they became friends and Yasuke was later given the prestigious rank of Samurai.

- Japan has over 50,000 people that are over 100 years old.
- Japan's Shinkansen high speed rail system has never had a fatal accident in nearly five decades of service.
- All of Japans highways have tolls, and it costs more than 300$ to travel across the country.
- In Japan, if you commit suicide by jumping in front of a Train, Rail Companies charge your family a fee.
- Japan and other countries have women-only sections in sky trains/subways to control and avoid groping activities from men.
- Russian and Japan still haven't signed a peace treaty to end World War II.

Jordan

- Petra in Jordan had a more efficient and advanced water system than ancient Rome, the system could support 40,000 people in a desert area.
- The current King of Jordan was an extra on Star Trek: Voyager, King Abdullah II of Jordan.
- Winston's Hiccup or Churchill's Sneeze is the huge zigzag in Jordan's eastern border with Saudi Arabia, supposedly because Winston Churchill drew the boundary of Jordan after a generous and lengthy lunch.

Kazakhstan

- Sacha Baron Cohen was nominated for an award in Kazakhstan for his role in Borat. According to the president, "He had raised the profile of the country to a level once thought impossible".
- There is a lake in Kazakhstan, Lake Chagan, which was created using a nuclear weapon and has decayed to the point that people can swim in it.
- Kazakhstan was the last nation to leave the Soviet Union on December 16, 1991, four days after Russia left.
- There is an underwater forest in Lake Kaindy, Kazakhstan that was created after an earthquake in 1911 that triggered a large landslide blocking the gorge and forming a natural dam.
- Wikitravel specifically warns visitors to Kazakhstan not to mention Borat.
- Lake Balkhash in Kazakhstan is divided by a strait into two distinct parts. What makes it very interesting is that the western part is fresh water while the Eastern part of the same lake is saline.
- Kazakhstan is the largest landlocked country in the world. It is larger than all of Western Europe.
- Kazakhstan is the world's largest producer of Uranium - 33.2% of the world's Uranium comes from there.

- Soviet Union deported almost all of its Korean population to Kazakhstan during the 1930s due to fear of Japanese espionage.

Kenya

- Farmers in Kenya are using elephants' natural fears of bees and building "beehive fences" that keep wild elephants from trampling the crops. It keeps the farms safe, and prevents farmers having to kill elephants to defend their livelihood.
- Almost three quarters of all of Kenya's athletics come from one tribe, the Kalenjins.
- Masai tribe in Kenya gave 14 cows to America after hearing about the 9/11 attacks.
- There is a hotel in Kenya that also serves as a giraffe sanctuary, and the giraffes stick their heads into the windows to get snacks at breakfast time.
- A Peace Corps project called No Sex for Fish gives women in Kenya their own fishing boats; otherwise they'd be expected to have sex with fishermen for the best catches to sell at market. HIV infection among beach communities there runs upwards of 30%.
- The British originally offered Kenya to Zionists as a Jewish homeland in 1903.
- Kenya has only won a single gold medal at the Olympics that was not in athletics, gold in boxing in 1988 at Seoul; in athletics they have 24 gold medals.

Kiribati

- Kiribati is the first country that will be entirely lost to rising sea levels and the government is already planning the complete, permanent evacuation of its population.
- Kiribati only has 1 registered taxi driver.
- Kiribati is the only country that falls in all four hemispheres.
- This Pacific island nation is pronounced 'kiribas'.
- During a two-hour period between 10:00 and 11:59 (UTC) each day, three different calendar days are in use. This means that when it's 11 p.m. Monday in Baker Island (USA), it's 1 a.m. Wednesday in Christmas Island (Kiribati) which makes for a 26 hour difference.
- Kiribati, locating in UTC+14, is the first place to begin a new day.

North Korea

- North Korea uses a fax machine to send threats to South Korea.
- The year is 103 (2014 in Europe), because North Korea marks years from the birth of Kim Il-sung, not Jesus.
- There are only two countries in the world Coca-Cola is not officially sold: North Korea and Cuba.

- North Korea enlists around 2000 women as part of a 'Pleasure Squad'. These are attractive women who provide entertainment and sexual services for top officials. One defector says Kim Jong-Il was "sentimental when drunk, and even shed tears".
- In North Korea you are forced to choose one of 28 government-approved haircuts.
- North Korea has its own airline, which also happens to be the only 1 star rated airline according to Skytrax.
- North Korea holds elections every 5 years in which the ballots list only one candidate.
- The largest stadium in the world, Rŭngnado May First Stadium, is located in Pyongyang. In the late 90's it was used as a venue to publicly burn several army generals that were implicated in an assassination attempt on Kim Jong-Il.
- Until 1972, North Korea's official capital was Seoul, in South Korea, because they always planned to retake the south.
- For 20 years the tallest "hotel" in the world was a 105-story empty pyramid in North Korea. It never opened and it remains as the tallest building in Pyongyang.
- Literacy in North Korea is defined by the ability to write "Kim Il-Sung".
- Every North Korean household and business is outfitted with a government-controlled radio that cannot be turned off, only turned down.

South Korea

- Under current South Korean laws, if a war breaks out, South Korea doesn't want to control its own military instead it wants the Americans to tell them what to do.
- South Korea bans children aged under 16 from playing online games between midnight and 6AM under a so-called "Cinderella Law".
- In South Korea, earning an Olympic Medal means you avoid a mandatory two-year military service.
- In South Korea 81% of middle and high schools prohibit relationships among students.
- Constitution of South Korea applies to all Koreans, so any North Koreans who manage to defect get citizenship.
- The militarized border between North and South Korea, with practically no human inhabitants, has become a refuge for multiple endangered species.
- Employers in South Korea give their workers a "kimchi bonus" in the fall so they can buy all the ingredients to make their annual supply.
- In South Korea there is a sex theme park called Love Land and features 140 sculptures representing humans in various sexual positions.

- Two companies represent 35 percent of South Korea's GDP: Samsung (23%) and Hyundai (12%).
- 21% of the population in South Korea uses the surname Kim.

Kosovo

- As a condition of Serbia's acceptance of increased sovereignty for Kosovo, Kosovo's official name was changed to "Kosovo*", the first and only state in history to have an asterisk as part of its name.
- Tonibler is a male given name in Kosovo, given in honor of former British Prime Minister Tony Blair following his role in the 1999 NATO air campaign against the Federal Republic of Yugoslavia during the Kosovo War.
- Pristina, the capital of Kosovo, has both a major road named after and a 10 ft. tall statue of President Bill Clinton as a token of appreciation for the US involvement in Kosovo's struggle against Yugoslavia.

Kuwait

- At the end of the Gulf War, 20 people died in Kuwait due to falling bullets from celebratory gunfire.
- The drive-through line on the opening day at the McDonald's restaurant in Kuwait City, Kuwait was estimated in seven miles long.
- After the 1990 Iraqi invasion of Kuwait, the Kuwait-Iraq barrier was constructed by the United Nations Security Council to prevent future invasion by Iraq. The separation barrier is a miles-long, deep trench and is guarded by hundreds of soldiers, and helicopters.
- Kuwait was formed by Britain to obstruct Arab nationalism. Taking away Iraq's major access to ports made Iraqi oil expensive to sell, causing oppression and angry leaders.
- In the aftermath of the Gulf War, Kuwait expelled 443,000 Palestinians from the country, about 30% of Kuwait's population.
- According to the CIA world Factbook, Kuwait had a budget surplus of 29% of their GDP in 2013, the biggest in the world.

Kyrgyzstan

- In Kyrgyzstan, "bride kidnapping" is a common practice where two or more men literally abduct a young woman from her home or in public and force her to marry one of them. It was made illegal in 1994 but is not enforced and is still being practiced.
- During WWII the Nazis made a giant swastika out of living trees in Kyrgyzstan, and it is still there today.
- There's a "Vladimir Putin Peak" in Tian-Shian Mountains in Kyrgyzstan.

Laos

- The eastern part of Laos was so heavily bombed that most people can supplement their income by collecting scrap metal 40 years later, some people completely rely on it.
- More explosive ordnance (bombs) were dropped on Laos by the US during the Vietnam War, than were dropped in the entirety of WWII, on both sides. Laos was hit by an average of one B- 52 bomb load every eight minutes, 24 hours a day, between 1964 and 1973.
- Non-marital sexual relationships between foreigners and Laotian citizens are illegal (in Laos).
- There is an area in Laos called "The Plain of Jars". A large area of the country full of huge, ancient jars all hewn from stone and no one is sure what they were made for.

Latvia

- In 1939, Latvia ordered 30 Hurricane fighters and paid for them. However, due to the start of the Second World War in September 1939, the aircraft were never delivered.
- Prostitutes in Latvia have to get their health checked monthly against STD infections.
- In Latvia you have to pay 7 euros ($9.5) for airport security check-in as they decided not to finance it from the state budget.
- There is a town in Latvia called "Ogre".
- The tiny and somewhat obscure Duchy of Courland (today part of Latvia) used to have a colonial empire including the Caribbean island of Tobago and Kunta Kinteh Island in the Gambia.
- There is a national holiday called Bear Slayer's Day in Latvia which commemorates Latvia's war veterans.

Lebanon

- In 2013, Lebanon had a population growth rate of 10%; the highest in the world, the high number can be explained due to Syrian refugees.
- In Lebanon governance, the President must be a Christian, the Prime Minister a Sunni, and the Speaker of Parliament a Shi'a.
- With evidence suggesting habitation since 8000 BCE, Byblos is considered the longest continuously inhabited city on the world.
- Rape is allowed in Lebanon as long as the rapist agrees to marry his victim.
- In Lebanon, if a man is caught having sex with a male animal then the penalty is death; sex with a female animal is ok.
- Syria does not recognize Lebanon as an independent country, believing that it should be part of "Greater Syria".

- There is a small forest in Lebanon (about 400 trees) named the Cedars of God, it was mentioned in the bible over 70 times and it was prized by historical figures such as Herod, Alexander, and Julius Caesar.

Lesotho

- Lesotho is the only country on Earth to lie completely above 1000m in elevation.
- Lesotho gets all of its power from renewable sources.
- Lesotho is a completely surrounded by South Africa.
- 23.6% of the population of Lesotho is HIV positive, one of the highest prevalence's in the world.
- Lesotho and Swaziland are the only countries where male life expectancy is higher than female.

Liberia

- In Monrovia a man with a 'blackboard blog' brings up-to-date information to people. For over 10 years, he has used a public bulletin board and painstakingly written out the day's news for all to see, all at no charge. He has an audience of over 10,000 readers.
- Liberia was established by citizens of the United States as a colony for former African American slaves and their free black descendants.
- In 1927 Charles King, President of Liberia won an election with 234,000 votes. The problem was, there were only 15,000 registered voters.
- During the Great Depression Senator Theodore G.Bilbo proposed to deport 12 million black Americans to Liberia at federal expense to relieve unemployment, Liberia had a population of 750.000.
- Former slaves immigrated from the U.S. to Liberia to create a "free state". However, the former U.S. slaves would also enslave the indigenous populations of Liberia. Only abolishing slavery in the 1930s.
- In 1914, Liberia was one of the two independent countries in Africa.

Libya

- The highest recorded temperature on Earth was 136°F (57.8°C) in 1922 in Aziziya, Libya.
- Libya is the hottest country in the world.
- Khadaffi, the former supreme leader of Libya, had an all-female squad of bodyguards.
- Cars in Libya can be rented or purchased with a camel sensing device.
- Libya was the only nation with a flag that was only a solid color, with no insignia or design. From 1977 to 2011 Libya's flag was just a plain green rectangle.

- The Greek colony of Cyrene in Libya, had an economy based largely on the export of Silphium, a plant so popular for use in abortions in the Ancient World that it was harvested to extinction.
- Tripoli, capital of Libya, is so-called because in ancient times the area was divided into three separate cities: "Land of three cities" in Greek is "Tripolitania".
- Libya has 75% of known oil reserves in Northern Africa, estimated to be 47.3 billion barrels of oil, which represents $4 trillion in the ground.
- On March 16, 1998, Libya was the first country to issue an arrest warrant for Osama Bin Laden.
- The first bomb ever recorder, was dropped in Lybia, more than 100 years ago.

Liechtenstein

- Despite not having a single medal in summer Olympics, it has 9 medals in the Winter Olympics.
- The average citizen of Liechtenstein doesn't even lock their door because crime in the country is low.
- During Liechtenstein's last military engagement in 1886, none of the 80 soldiers sent were injured, and in fact, 81 returned, including a new Italian "friend".
- Until 1936, Liechtenstein and Haiti were unknowingly using the same flag, and they didn't find out until they competed against each other in the Olympics.
- Liechtenstein, one of the smallest countries in the world, has one of the lowest business and corporate tax rates, highest GDP per capita, zero external debt, and more registered businesses than people.
- The Swiss army accidentally invaded the Liechtenstein, two times. On 5 December 1985, rockets fired by the Swiss Army landed in Liechtenstein, causing a forest fire, compensation was paid. On 13 October 1992, following written orders, Swiss Army cadets unknowingly crossed the border and went to Triesenberg to set up an observation post. In 2007, Swiss troops accidentally invaded the Liechtenstein territory after getting lost in a rain storm.
- You can rent the country of Liechtenstein for only $70,000 a night, complete with customized street signs and your own temporary currency.
- Despite being one of the richest countries in the world (by GDP per capita) Liechtenstein does not have an airport and ranks as one of the least visited tourist destinations in the world.
- Liechtenstein is one of the two countries that are doubly landlocked. A country is said to be "doubly landlocked" if it is surrounded only by other landlocked countries.

- Liechtenstein (with only 36k citizens) is the world's largest producer and exporter of dentures.
- Technically, Liechtenstein is still at war with Germany as Bismarck deemed it too small to sign a peace treaty with it back in 1866.
- Liechtenstein only gave women the vote in 1984.
- Liechtenstein and the Czech Republic did not recognize each other as sovereign states until 2009, due to a land dispute in the Czech territory.
- Liechtenstein has 87 police officers, for a population of almost 37,000.

Lithuania

- There is a small district of Vilnius, Lithuania that has declared itself an independent republic. It has its own flag, currency, president, cabinet, and an army of 11 men.
- There is a theme park in Vilnius where you can spend two hours reliving the communist occupation. Former members of the Soviet army will teach you the Soviet anthem, interrogate you and even give you a shot of vodka when it's all over.
- Until 2002, women in Lithuania were required to undergo a gynecological examination before receiving their driver's license to make sure they aren't suffering from any "female illnesses".
- There is an annual Baby Racing competition in order to find the 'Fastest Crawler in the country'.
- Basketball is so popular in Lithuania that it is sometimes referred to as "the second religion of Lithuania".
- There's a "Hill of Crosses" in Lithuania with over 100,000 crosses of various sizes, from centimeters to several meters tall.

Luxembourg

- Luxembourg's gold medal at the 1952 Olympics was so unexpected that the organizers had neglected to give the band a score for their national anthem. The musicians hurriedly improvised a tune which bore little resemblance to the Luxembourg anthem.
- In Luxembourg you must be trilingual (French, German, and Luxembourgish) to graduate secondary school.
- Luxembourg's education system is trilingual: the first years of primary school are in Luxembourgish, before changing to German, while in secondary school, the language of instruction changes to French.
- Luxembourg has the highest GDP vs. external debt ratio, with its debt exceeding its GDP by 3443%. This is due to the size of the banking system in the country.

- Approximately 16.1% of Luxembourg's population is Portuguese. This makes them one of the largest ethnic groups as a proportion of the total national population.
- There is a graveyard in Luxembourg, where American soldiers (Including George S. Patton) have white cross headstones, while a graveyard for German soldiers nearby has dark cross headstones.
- In Argentina there's an observatory larger than the entire country of Luxembourg.
- The minimum wage in Luxembourg is 1,801.49 Euros or 2,214.50 USD per month.

Macedonia

- Greece doesn't want the Republic of Macedonia to use the name "Macedonia" without a geographic qualifier (like "Northern") because Greece has its own Macedonian regions. The conflict transcends into the use of symbols historically belonging to Greece, and the claim to Alexander the Great.
- In Macedonia a head nod indicates "no", contrary to the gesture's meaning in most other areas of the world.

Madagascar

- The "Madagascar Plan" was a proposal of the Third Reich to relocate the Jewish population of Europe to the island of Madagascar.
- Madagascar was first settled by people from Borneo (which is over 4000 miles away), not Africa (250 miles away).
- The language spoken in Madagascar isn't related to African languages but instead is very similar to Malay, spoken in a country 6500 km away.
- 90% of the wildlife on Madagascar is found nowhere else on the planet.
- Madagascar is about 1.6 times bigger than Japan.
- In some tribes when a boy turns five in Madagascar, it is a ritual that they circumcise him, and then a male member of the family must eat the foreskin.
- Weavers in Madagascar created an 11'x4'(335cmx121cm) tapestry made entirely out of spider's silk.
- Madagascar got its name when Marco Polo mistakenly thought he was in Mogadishu, Somalia. He botched the spelling and the name stuck.
- Madagascar depicted in the DreamWorks Animation films as a region with no humans, actually has a population of over 22 million; greater than the populations of New Zealand, Denmark, Norway, and Ireland combined.

Malawi

- Malawi has a patient to doctor ratio of 88,321 to 1 which translates to 173 doctors for a population of over 15 million people.

- There are tobacco farms in Malawi where child laborers, as young as 5, are suffering severe physical symptoms from absorbing up to the equivalent of 50 cigarettes a day through their skin.
- Malawi president Bingu WA Mutharika vacated his home, a 300-bedroom mansion, in 2005 believing it to be haunted.
- In the 1970's, the government of Malawi explicitly denied entry to "'hippies' and men with long hair and flared trousers".
- In January 2011, the Malawi Minister of Justice, George Chaponda, said that Air Fouling Legislation would make public farting illegal in his country.

Malaysia

- Blowjobs are illegal in Malaysia and it is punishable with imprisonment of 20 years maximum and whipping.
- Toyota Altis ads featuring Brad Pitt were banned in Malaysia after the country's deputy information minister ruled that Pitt's handsome appearance may make Malaysian countrymen feel inferior.
- The movie Zoolander was banned in Malaysia due to its negative connotation about the country's poverty level, dependence on sweatshops, and the plot to kill the prime minister of Malaysia.
- The McDonald's in Malaysia has delivery service.
- Possession of 7oz (200g) of Marijuana in Malaysia is an automatic death penalty.
- Malaysia is the first and only country that allows people to travel to North Korea without a visa. In 2013, Kim Jong-Un received an honorary doctorate from a Malaysia University.
- Under the Sharia law in Malaysia, a Muslim man can legally divorce his wife by text-messaging her.
- Anal sex is illegal in Malaysia, even among consenting adults.
- There is a village in Malaysia that, as revenge for killing humans, captures tiger sharks, stuffs their mouths with poisonous sea urchins, and releases them so they die a slow painful death.
- 90% of the income tax in Malaysia is paid by overseas Chinese who make up less than a quarter of the population.
- The UK once air dripped crates of cats into Borneo, Malaysia to help with the rat infestation they were having.
- Monarchies in Malaysia rotate the throne between different Branches of the Royal Families.
- In Malaysia, taxi drivers use pandan leaves as a cockroach repellent in their vehicles.
- In Malaysia the body mass index (BMI) of students is listed on their report cards, and unhealthy food is banned from school canteens.

- Malaysia is the largest condom producing country in the world. Malaysia also bans abortion with exception "for maternal life, health, and/or mental health".

Maldives

- The president of Maldives has begun buying land in India for his citizens, preparing for when the Maldives Archipelago will be flooded due to global warming in a few decades.
- The world's first undersea restaurant is in the Maldives.
- In Maldives, open practice of any religion except Islam is forbidden and liable to prosecution. Furthermore a non-Muslim may not become a citizen of the Maldives. Maldives is the only country where all citizens must practice Islam and there is no freedom of religion.
- The island nation of the Maldives' highest point is 2.4m (7.8 feet) above sea level.
- The island nation Maldives is home to the world's biggest island of trash. The artificially created landfill receives 330 tons of trash a day and its size is growing by a square meter a day. The island is an increasingly serious ecological and health problem in the Maldives. This is also the reason Maldives look so clean, they dump all of their garbage in Thilafushi.
- The capital city of Maldives, Male which houses 100,000 people over 1 square mile making it one of the most densely populated cities on Earth, even denser than New Delhi or Mexico City.

Mali

- Mali has the lowest literacy rate for men, with only 36% of the male population reading and writing. The female population has a literacy rate of 20%.
- Since 2012 until now it has the second biggest fertility rate with an average of 7 births per woman.
- Emperor Musa I of Mali (1280-1337, West Africa) was the richest person of all time (estimated wealth $ 400 billion). He gave away so much gold during his pilgrimage to Mecca in 1324 that the cities of Cairo, Medina and Mecca suffered from severe inflation for the next decade.
- The preferred ringtone for al-Qaeda influenced militants in Mali is a laughing baby because it is not music and also is family-friendly.
- There is a mosque in Mali made entirely out of mud.
- Mali is the third largest producer of Gold in Africa. Major mines in Mali are owned by British and Australian and French companies.
- Timbuktu, as in the saying "From here to Timbuktu", is a city in the African country of Mali, and located in the Sahara Desert.

Malta

- During WW2 three bombs hit a church in Malta, two "bounced off" and did not explode and one pierced the church, landing among a congregation of 300, but did not explode.
- There is a 5000 year old underground temple in Malta that was discovered by accident containing 6000 skeletons.
- During the Siege of Malta in 1565, 6,000 knights defeated 30,000 Turkish invaders with primitive flamethrowers and hundreds of burning hula hoops. During the Ottoman siege of Malta over 130,000 cannonballs were fired towards defenders and citizens for four hot summer months. A third of the defenders and population of Malta perished but they withstood the siege. The Ottomans never again attempted to take the island.
- The cross on the flag of Malta is the honorary George Cross, granted to Malta by the British king because of their bravery in WW2.
- Malta imports 87% of their water supplies.
- Malta has its own language, Maltese; it is based on Arabic grammar with mostly Italian and English vocabulary.
- A land less organization called The Sovereign Military Order of Malta is a sovereign entity in international law, with diplomatic missions to 92 countries and permanent missions to the UN, the European Commission and other international and multinational organizations.
- In Malta, Play Mobil makes 2 million figures every week, five times the island's total human population, while no Play Mobil figures are made in China.

Marshall Islands

- Bikini Bottom's location is found underneath Bikini Atoll, Marshall Islands. Two-piece bathing suits received the name "Bikini" after the atoll in the Marshall Islands, where the U.S. tested nuclear weapons in the '30s and '40s, due to the reaction people had to seeing both the bathing suit and the bomb detonation for the first time.
- Tropical Storm 'Zelda', in 1991, destroyed 95% of Marshall Islands' crops.
- The Marshall Islands skipped an entire day in 1993 to join eastern side of the International Date Line.

Mauritania

- Mauritania tried to ban slavery thrice, in 1905, 1981, and as latest as August 2007. It is the 'last stronghold' of slavery on earth with 20% of the population being "slave".
- Female obesity is considered so attractive in Mauritania that 75 percent of rural Mauritanian girls are forcibly fattened on camel milk and animal fat in a

custom called "leblouh". Some women in Mauritania force-feed their daughters because obesity for women is idealized in the country.

- In Mauritania, a woman's size indicates the space she occupies in her husband's heart. To make sure no other woman can ever have room, girls are sent to special farms where older women will administer the necessary diet. Their daily consumption comes up to a whopping 16,000 calories, eight times more than the usual.
- Mauritania banned the use of plastic bags to protect the lives of animals because they used to die after eating them.

Mauritius

- The National Animal of Mauritius is the extinct Dodo.
- In 2013 Mauritius was the only country in Africa currently ranked as a full democracy by The Economist.

Mexico

- In Mexico the act of escaping from prison is considered legal because the law recognizes that all people have a fundamental desire to be free.
- Illegal immigration from Mexico to the U.S. has decreased by 80% since 2000.
- In 1938 Mexico was the only country to protest against the German annexation of Austria.
- In 1838, France and Mexico fought the Pastry War over Mexico's refusal to pay 600,000 pesos to a French pastry chef whose shop had been ransacked by Mexican officers.
- 75% of all sesame seeds grown in Mexico end up on McDonald's hamburger buns.
- There are more Americans living in Mexico City than Wyoming.
- Mexico sent 300,000 workers to U.S. farms and factories to help with the Allied war effort in WWII.
- Cinco de Mayo is a bigger deal in the US then it is in Mexico.
- The staple ingredient in most Italian foods is not native to Italy or Europe. The tomato originated in Mexico.
- Mexico is the biggest exporter of beer in the world. Their big neighbor, US is the biggest importer.
- Senators in Mexico cannot immediately run for re-election and thus, the Senate is completely renewed every six years.
- There is an ancient city in central Mexico that no one knows the origin of, even today. The Aztecs called it "the city of the gods" because they claimed it was built overnight by the gods because it wasn't there one day and was the next.

- One major reason Texas declared independence from Mexico was because Mexico abolished slavery, and Texans viewed it as an infringement on their liberty.
- Mexico City has more museums than any other city in the world.
- The world's wealthiest man, Mexico's Carlos Slim, accounts for roughly 5% of his entire country's economic output.
- If you are in an auto accident in Mexico, police may detain you until they determine liability and your ability to pay any penalties.
- The official name of Mexico is The United Mexican States.
- The 10 most dangerous cities on Earth are in Latin America, 5 of which are in Mexico.
- Mexico drinks more Coca-Cola per capita than any other country in the world, including the US.
- The biggest pyramid by volume and the largest monument ever constructed anywhere in the world is the Great Pyramid of Cholula in Mexico.
- In 1917, the Germans sent a telegraph to the Mexicans asking them to declare war on the US, if the US declared war on Germany. Germany promised Mexico financial aid and all land lost in the Mexican/American War.

Micronesia

- The megalithic ruins of a city known as Nan Madol exist in Micronesia.
- There is an island in Micronesia that uses giant circular stones up to 12 feet in diameter as currency for marriages, inheritance, political deals, ransom of the battle dead, and even for food. The Island of Yap, Micronesia use Rai stones as currency and these stones can be huge, the largest are 3.65 meters / 12 feet in diameter, 1.5 ft. thick and weigh 4 metric tons (8,800 lb.).
- The fattest country in the world is Micronesia.
- The world's smallest congress/parliament is in Micronesia, with just 14 MPs.

Moldova

- In 2003 a Moldovan-Romanian dictionary published in Moldova has become a bestseller even though Moldovan and Romanian are basically the same language. It was described by leading scholars as an absurdity.
- In 1997, the United States purchased 21 MiG-29 fighter aircraft (made by Russia) from the former Soviet country of Moldova.

Monaco

- Monaco is the country with a higher population density, with 48,000 people per square mile or 18,000 people per square kilometer. It has a total of 37,000 people condensed in only a small territory.
- The average life expectancy for a woman in Monaco is 93.71.

- A leisurely stroll around the border of Monaco would take about 40 minutes.
- The nation that is least successful in Olympics is Monaco; it participated in 27 winter and summer Olympics games and hasn't won a single medal.
- Monaco eliminated income tax in 1869 because the revenue of the casino was sufficient to sustain the principality's government.
- The citizens of Monaco are forbidden from entering the gaming rooms of the Monte Carlo Casino. Passports are checked at the door to enforce this rule.
- The Principality of Monaco has a 0.0% unemployment rate.
- Before the Monaco F1 race, manhole covers are welded down. That's because the down force created by an F1 car has enough suction to rip them off.
- There have been two different times at the Monaco Grand Prix where a Formula One driver has gone off course and plunged into the Ocean. Both drivers survived their respective incidents.
- Central Park is almost twice as large as the country of Monaco.
- France annexed 95% of Monaco territory in the Franco-Monegasque Treaty of 1861.

Mongolia

- Mongolia is the country with the lowest population density in the world, with only 1.76 people per square kilometer or 4.56 per square mile. Still it is higher than Alaska (1.3 per mi2 or 1.3 per km2).
- Mongolia's navy consists of a tugboat manned by 7 people, only one of whom can swim.
- There is a place in Mongolia that was declared sacred by Genghis Khan. The only people allowed to enter were the Mongol Royal Family and a tribe of elite warriors, the darkhat, whose job it was to guard it, punishment for entering being death. They carried out their task for 697 years, until 1924.
- In Mongolia, if your foot taps against someone else's, it is respectful to immediately shake hands with them.
- When completed, a single mine in Mongolia is expected to account for 30% of the entire nation's GDP.
- Mongolia has an extremely young population, with over 70 percent of people being less than thirty years old.
- Ulan Bator, the capital of Mongolia, is the coldest national capital in the world.
- There are twice as many Mongolians in China (5.9 Million) as there are in Mongolia (2.9 Million).
- Mongolia is the largest exporter of Animal Hair.

Montenegro

- When Montenegro became independent from Yugoslavia, its Internet domain name went from being .yu to .me.

- Due to a diplomatic irregularity, the Principality of Montenegro and Japan were at war from 1904 to 2006.
- Every year in northwest Montenegro there is a competition in laying. Rules state that sitting or standing is disallowed. Who keeps laying the longest wins 300€.
- Montenegro auctions off all of their .me web addresses as Premium pun sites. See websites as hate.me, leave.me.

Morocco

- Morocco, in December 1777, became the first nation to recognize the United States, and together they maintain the United States' longest unbroken treaty.
- In 2003, Morocco offered to send 2,000 monkeys to assist the war effort in Iraq. They were to be used to detonate land mines.
- The oldest existing and continually operating educational institution in the world is a university in Morocco (University of al-Karaouine). It is older than Oxford, since it was founded by a woman, Fatima Muhammad Al-Fihri, in 859 AD. Its reputation attracted a future Pope, Gerbert of Auvergne, who brought the basis of our current way of representing numbers, Arabic numerals, back to Europe with him.
- The world's largest film studio is located in Morocco consisting mostly of deserts and mountains and was used for Game of Thrones episodes, The Mummy, Gladiator etc. It has also become a popular tourist resort due to the remaining sets of old movie productions.
- Morocco is the only country located on the African continent that is not part of the African Union. Morocco withdrew because the Western Sahara was recognized as its own state and not a part of Morocco.
- In Morocco, it is a criminal offence to possess a Christian Bible written in the Arabic language.
- The oldest U.S. embassy is in Morocco. As testament to the special nature of the U.S.-Moroccan relationship, the Moroccan city of Tangier is home to the oldest U.S. diplomatic property in the world, and the only building on foreign soil that is listed in the U.S. National Register of Historic Places, the American Legation in Tangier.

Mozambique

- In 1982, 900 children from Mozambique went to East Germany to complete their secondary education and become the new socialist elite leaders of Mozambique. The Problem was when they returned in 1988, the Mozambique was no longer a socialist country.

- When Mozambique gained independence in 1975, the remainders of the country's 250,000 Portuguese inhabitants were given 24 hours to leave and were only allowed 20kg of luggage.
- The flag of Mozambique has an AK-47 on it; the AK-47 is featured in the flag of Mozambique as a testament to its role in the present government's seizure of power.
- The first record of foreign samurai is Yasuke, a former slave from Mozambique who came to Japan as a servant to a Jesuit priest in 1579 but befriended the local warlord and fought alongside him in Honnō-ji.
- Most children in Mozambique are not named until Age 1, because so few survive.
- Mozambique has the lowest rate of Gross national saving (includes personal saving, plus business saving, plus government saving), with a negative value of 5.6%. One of the only six countries that has a negative value.

Myanmar (Burma)

- The Myanmar Securities Exchange Centre is the only stock exchange in Burma (Myanmar), and has had only two listings since its founding in 1996.
- Burma (Myanmar) has left hand traffic; despite most cars are being right hand drive. This happened in 1970 after military administration of Ne Win decreed that traffic would drive on the right hand side of the road after being advised by his astrologer, who had said "move to the right".
- The biggest bell ever cast has been lying at the bottom of a river in Myanmar for the last 400 years.
- It is not certain, but according to some news, Myanmar leads the world, with 26% at the most on military budgets as a percent of GDP.

Namibia

- The Skeleton Coast of Namibia, aka "The Gates of Hell", is a place so inhospitable that when the MV Dunedin went aground in 1942, passengers were only rescued after another ship ran aground, a big aircraft was damaged on landing, was repaired and crashed again, and several army trucks were lost.
- The largest naturally occurring iron mass on the Earth's surface was discovered in 1920 on a small farm in rural Namibia. Unusual for its size, over 60 tons, it was found to be extraterrestrial in origin, proving to be the largest iron meteorites to ever reach the Earth's surface intact.
- There is a 1500 km band of land in Namibia covered in unexplained "Fairy Circles" that appear to grow and also die. Scientists have studied the area for over 30 years and still do not know their cause.
- The Herero tribe of Namibia still wear clothing reminiscent the Victorian style of the German occupants who once tried to wipe them out.

- The Namibian Constitution actually calls to preserve the health of its ecosystem/environment. This is one of the main factors to why Namibia is so untouched by industrialization.
- Namibia's name is derived from Namib, which means "area where there is nothing" in the Nama language.

Nauru

- It is not certain which is the fattest country on the world; Nauru with over 70% of its population being obese may be the fattest country in the world. Some sources state that 97% of men and 93% of women are overweight or obese and over 40% of the population suffers from type 2 diabetes.
- The nation of Nauru, population 9000, was once the richest nation in the world by GDP per capita thanks to its rich phosphate deposits formed by bird droppings.
- Nauru, which recently had one of the top GDPs per capita worldwide, is now one of the poorest, with a 90% unemployment rate. They were living off the resources; strip mined it all and squandered the savings.
- The island nation of Nauru (pop. 9,322) was paid $50M by Russia to recognize the breakaway republics of South Ossetia and Abkhazia, making it the 4th country to do so. They were also paid $130M by Taiwan to establish diplomatic relations, and now Taiwan has the only embassy in Nauru.
- Nauru, being a tiny island nation in the pacific, is the least visited country in the world.
- Nauru is the smallest independent nation in the world that speaks its own language, Nauruan.
- The single island Republic of Nauru is the smallest country to have its own national airline which flies to places like Australia and Fiji the island state Nauru operates one Boeing 737, which costs them 30% of their GDP.

Nepal

- The latest reports state that the Nepal government charges $25,000 USD to climb to the upper base camp of Mount Everest.
- Nepal was the first country in Asia to introduce gay marriage. It has also outlawed the death penalty.
- On 1st of June 2001 the heir to the Nepalese throne, Prince Dipendra, shot and killed several members of the royal family, while intoxicated, including his parents, the reigning King and Queen. This eventually led to the abolishment of the Kingdom of Nepal.
- The flag of Nepal is the only flag in the world that isn't a quadrilateral.
- The airport most used to get to Mount Everest in Nepal is also most dangerous airport in the world. A 1500 foot / 450 meters runway at over 9000 foot / 2500 meters elevation with 7 crashes in past ten years.

- The Mustang district of Nepal did not allow any outsiders to enter until 1991. Even after 1991, a special permit is needed and costs $700 per person for 10 days.
- Threats from rebels and royalty in Nepal made it so hard to find candidates for the 2006 elections, that opponents strapped signs to stray dogs that said "Vote for Me" as a form of satire.
- In old Hindu traditions in Nepal, there was three months of prison for killing a pedestrian, but a life imprisonment/death penalty for killing a cow.
- Most of the Sherpa people in Nepal have the same last name because government workers didn't bother asking their clan names.
- Nepal has 8 of the 10 tallest mountains in the world in it, including Mount Everest.
- In Nepal their goddess is a little girl who has to meet a strict criteria including never losing blood.
- The most deadly mountain in the world is Annapurna in Nepal, claiming 41% of the climbers who attempt to summit.
- Nepal has had 21 prime ministers in the last 24 years.

The Netherlands

- The Netherlands has been sending Canada 10,000 tulips every year for the past 70 years in appreciation for the liberation of the Netherlands from Nazi forces.
- During one special day in 1940 a section of a hospital in Ottawa became international territory so a Dutch Princess could be born a full Dutch citizen, which was a requirement to be a Dutch Princess.
- There is a fake village with fake shops and restaurants that is actually a care home for elderly dementia sufferers in the Netherlands.
- The IKEA HQ in Delft, Netherlands had to stop offering their €1 breakfast during the weekends because the highways couldn't handle the traffic it attracted.
- The crown princess of the Netherlands goes to a public school.
- One of the longest wars in history, between the Netherlands and the Isles of Scilly, lasted from 1651 to 1986. There were no casualties.
- The largest mountain in The Netherlands is located in the Caribbean.
- The rather small country of the Netherlands is the 2nd largest exporter of agricultural goods behind the USA, with exports earning $79 billion in 2013. They export two thirds of the world's fresh-cut plants, flowers, and flower bulbs.
- Netherlands is constructing special bridges for wildlife in order to connect habitats and keep animals from being hit by cars.
- Giethoorn is a town in the Netherlands with no roads. Only canals, sidewalks, and bike paths.

- The Netherlands may be at a war with water, they have to constantly pump water, usually with windmills, back into the North Sea, or else it could engulf the entire country.
- There is a US law that allows the US to invade the Netherlands to protect American military personnel if they are being detained by the International Criminal Court in The Hague.

New Zealand

- It is illegal in New Zealand for airport security to use any device which would produce images of a person without their clothes on.
- New Zealand is part of a 93% submerged continent known as Zealandia.
- There was a dolphin named Pelorus Jack that regularly guided ships in New Zealand through treacherous waters until his disappearance in 1912.
- In 1996, a deranged man stormed into a New Zealand radio station, took the manager hostage and issued one demand, the station play Rainbow Connection by Kermit the Frog.
- The logo of the Royal New Zealand Air Force is the kiwi, a flightless bird.
- New Zealand will deny people residency visas if they have too high of a BMI and there has been cases of people rejected because of their weight.
- In June 1984 the prime minister of New Zealand, Robert Muldoon, drunkenly announced on national television that a snap election was to be held in a month's time. With 93.7% of voters turning out for the election, he lost. The occasion is sometimes remembered as the 'Schnapps election'.
- According to a book on New Zealand farming, Moscow offered to give New Zealand a nuclear submarine, MiG jets and tanks to help settle Russia's debt for dairy products. When told that NZ had a nuclear-free policy, Moscow's response was: "tie it up in some port and connect it to the national grid".
- New Zealand has over 70% power generation from renewable sources with a target to hit 90% by 2025.
- Japan has the most vending machines in the world (5.52 million) which is more than the population of New Zealand.

Nicaragua

- Nicaragua invaded Costa Rica in 2010, because of a misplaced border on Google Maps.
- In October/2014 Nicaragua has granted a Hong Kong company permission to build a canal across the country, connecting the Pacific and Caribbean and competing against the Panama Canal. Construction is expected to begin in December 2014 and finish after six years.
- Honduras and Nicaragua almost went to war due to a stamp. The stamp had the border between Honduras and Nicaragua defined in a conflictual way.

- Managua (capital of Nicaragua) was once the most modern city in Central America. In 1972 90% of the city was destroyed in an Earthquake and has never fully recovered.
- A US southerner named William Walker took over Nicaragua in 1856 with a private army of 60 men, declared himself ruler, made slavery legal, and asked President Pierce to annex the territory. He was later executed by the Honduran authorities.
- Nicaragua has a festival, where men beat each other with dried up bull penis.

Niger

- Since 2012 until now it has the biggest fertility rate with an average of 7 births per woman, and an average of 47 births per 1,000 people.
- People from Niger are called Nigeriens while people from Nigeria are called Nigerians.
- Around 49.8% of Niger's population is between 0-14 years old.
- In 1995, Nigeria donated 88,000 doses of meningitis vaccine to its neighbor Niger, but before the authorities realized that these vaccines were fake, about 60 000 people had been "inoculated" with what could just be water.
- Slavery wasn't made a crime in Niger until 2003.
- The Wodaabe people in Niger have a courtship ritual where the men stand on tiptoe, bare their teeth, and roll their eyes to impress women.
- In 2004 the number of medics practicing in the Republic of Niger was under 400 while having a population of 11,360,540.

Nigeria

- In 1995, Nigeria donated 88,000 doses of meningitis vaccine to its neighbor Niger, but before the authorities realized that these vaccines were fake, about 60 000 people had been "inoculated" with what could just be water.
- Sesame Street in Nigeria has a version of Cookie Monster named Zobi the Yam Monster. Since not many Nigerian children have access to cookies, the producers decided to give Zobi an insatiable craving for one of the country's staple foods. He often shouts out, "Me eat yam!".
- Nigeria has overtaken Ireland in Guinness sales and is the number 2 consumer of Guinness worldwide.
- In 2005 in Northern Nigeria a group of Muslim leaders declared the polio vaccine to be a conspiracy to sterilize the true believers. Subsequently the disease began to spread again.
- In January/2014 a 2 mbps Internet Connection in Nigeria was costing $296/month.
- In the 1970s there was a Utopian village in Nigeria where there were no cemeteries because the villagers thought they were immortal.

- Nigeria produces more films each year than the United States and is second only to India. Informally, the cinema of Nigeria is referred to as Nollywood.
- Africa's biggest city, Lagos in Nigeria, has a population of 21 million and is quickly becoming one of the most populated cities in the world. It is also the biggest city in the world without metro lines.
- Since 2009, Nigeria is the leading importer of Andorran exports with a share of more than 50%. Mainly due food products.

Norway

- 99% of energy production in Norway is by hydroelectric generation plants, producing enough for home consumption and exporting.
- Norway once had to close a tunnel because it was full of burning cheese.
- Norway will allow any student from anywhere in the world to study at their Public Universities completely free of charge.
- Norway introduced salmon sushi to the Japanese to increase their salmon exports.
- Norway has very strict rules on advertising cars as "green", saying "cars can do nothing good for the environment except less damage than others".
- Norway has world's highest gas prices. Though they have oil reserves, they don't subsidize fuel and use the $ for free college education and national infrastructure.
- When you get a book published in Norway, the Norwegian Government will buy 1000 copies of our book and distribute them throughout the libraries of the country.
- The late King Olav V of Norway used public transport. He was nicknamed Folkekonge, "The people's king".
- Norway has no minimum wage, however McDonald's workers make between 95 - 140+ kroner ($16-24USD) per hour depending on their age.
- Penguins were once introduced in Norway; one of them was promptly shot by a Norwegian matron who claimed it was a freak of nature that had invaded her yard.
- In Norway you can return your library book anywhere in the country regardless of where it was loaned.
- The monarch of Norway's title is "Norway's King" rather than "King of Norway", signifying that he belongs to the country and not vice versa.
- In 1905 Norway voted 99.95% in favor of independence from Sweden and only 184 people opposed.

Oman

- Oman is home to the world's only camel-backed bagpipe military band.
- The city of Muscat, Oman has a solid red flag.
- In Oman it's illegal to drive a dirty car.

- Said bin Taimur, the Sultan of Oman, was skeptical of banks and investments so he kept all of his gold under his bed.
- Oman's leading corporate house founder Sheikh is actually the only Hindu Sheikh in the world who traces his roots to Indian state of Gujarat from where he set sails 143 years ago.

Pakistan

- A former bonded child laborer from Pakistan escaped the carpet factory at the age of 10, helped free over 3000 kids from slavery, helped bring down Pakistani carpet exports by $34 million, all that before being murdered at the age of 13.
- Pakistan's oldest brewery was established in 1860. Under Pakistani law, they cannot sell their products to Muslims, which represent 97% of the population, or export them outside of Pakistan.
- Pakistan is intolerant of gays, but has the highest search rates of gay porn on the Internet according to some sources.
- The Kalash tribe in Pakistan has a festival where a prepubescent boy is sent up to the mountains to live with goats for the Summer, and when he returns he is allowed to have sex with anyone woman for a 24 hour period, even another man's wife.
- Millions of spiders completely cocooned trees in silk after the unprecedented 2010 flooding in Pakistan.
- In 1951, Hindus constituted 22% of the Pakistani population. Today, the share of Hindus is down to 1.7% in Pakistan.
- Kite flying is banned in Pakistan's Punjab province because people use strings coated with glass or abrasive chemicals to slice the lines of 'rivals', in 2007 eleven people were killed in kite flying related incidents.
- The Partition of India created two Pakistans, East and West. In 1971, East Pakistan gained its independence and became Bangladesh.
- 80% of all balls used in football / soccer, are made in Pakistan, unfortunately many of them are made using child labor.
- Pakistan forbids its citizens from going to Israel by putting the legend 'This passport is valid for all countries of the World except Israel' on Pakistani passports.
- Pakistan was originally an acronym coined in 1933 referring to the 5 northern provinces of India; [P]unjab, North-West Frontier Province ([A]fghan Province), [K]ashmir, [S]ind, and Baluchis[tan].
- Pakistan is the only country that does not recognize Armenia.
- Farmers in mountainous Pakistan traditionally grow their own glaciers as a reliable water source.
- The 44 of 100 tallest mountains are in Pakistan.

Palau

- Palau has the largest ratio when comparing the capital population to the largest city. The biggest city, Koror (pop. 11,200), has 41 times more people than the capital, Ngerulmud, with only 271 people.
- There is a lake in the country of Palau where jellyfish evolved without stingers after the lake's connection to the sea closed, leaving them isolated from their natural predators. These 'Golden' jellyfish are totally harmless to humans and you can swim with them.
- In the 459 km2 nation of Palau, there exists 16 states, with the smallest, Hatohobei, being just 3 km2 in size, with a population of 44, yet having its own flag and language.
- Palau has clear visibility in its waters up to 200 feet deep.

Palestinian State*

- Palestine has never existed as a country, only as a geographic term.
- The residents of Palestine are called "Palestinians". Since Palestine includes both modern day Israel and Jordan, both Arab and Jewish residents of this area were referred to as "Palestinians".
- The Arab Population of British Mandatory Palestine didn't want to name the area "Palestine," but rather just "Southern Syria".
- The Palestinian state is recognized by more than 66% of the UN members.
- The term Palestine dates back to 1150 BC Egypt and has changed many times depending on who ruled the region.

Panama

- The average toll to pass through the Panama Canal is US$54,000 but it can cost over $300,000 for a cruise ship to pass through the Canal. The most expensive regular toll fee is US$375,600.
- Scotland attempted to colonize Panama in the hopes of creating an important international trading hub, through overland routes across the isthmus. The venture was disastrous, many of the colonists died, and Scotland lost as much as a third of its wealth.
- Panama gained independence from Colombia due to the United States interest in building the Panama Canal. In 1921 the United States compensated Colombia with US$25 million and a formal apology from US Congress for interfering with the separation of Panama from Colombia in 1903.
- The Pacific end of the Panama Canal is farther east than the Atlantic end.
- The "Valley of Square Trees" in Panama is the only known place in the world where trees have rectangular trunks.

- Panama has the world's largest merchant navy by number of registered vessels; it counted 6,413 merchant ships in 2010, more than double of the second place.
- Panama is the country with the smaller production of oil; it produces on average 2 barrels of oil a day.

Papua New Guinea

- There is a tribe in Papua New Guinea where the women ambush men for sex and can urinate on him and bite off his eyebrow and eyelashes if they aren't satisfied.
- Before the young boys of the Etoro tribe of Papua New Guinea can be called adults, they must consume the semen of their elders. Many tribes in Papua New Guinea require young males to perform oral sex on their elders in belief that ingesting their semen passes down their power.
- Papua New Guinea has a population of only 6.2 million yet is the most linguistically diverse place on earth with over 850 languages spoken and hundreds more dialects.
- There is a rare disease known as "Laughing Sickness" or "Kuru". It is spread among a tribe of cannibals in Papua New Guinea, contacted by eating a human body.
- In order to distinguish between evil sorcery and innocent sorcery, Papua New Guinea, introduced the 'Sorcery Act 1971'. The Act states "Some kinds of sorcery are practiced not for evil purposes but for innocent ones and it may not be necessary for the law to interfere with them".

Paraguay

- The Paraguayan War (1864-70) was proportionally the most devastating war in modern history, it left Paraguay with less than 20% of its prewar population and with a 1:4 male to female ratio. The Paraguayan War was so catastrophic for the male population of Paraguay, that there were only 26,000 adult men left alive in the country at the end of the war. In some areas, the female to male ratio in some areas were high as 20:1.
- Dueling is still legal in Paraguay provided that both parties are registered blood donors.
- The flag of Paraguay has two different sides.
- Paraguay produces nearly all its electricity from hydroelectric sources.
- The Itaipu Dam, Paraguay, is over 7km long and can shift 62 million liters of water a second.

Peru

- Yungay, Peru was the site of the deadliest avalanche in history. In 1962, two American scientists predicted the calamity, and were consequently forced to flee by the government. Eight years later, their prediction came true and 20,000 people were killed in a day.

- In Lima, Peru there is a billboard that creates drinkable water out of thin air.
- In 1600 a volcano eruption in Peru killed approximately 2 million in Russia. The Russian famine of 1601–1603 was Russia's worst famine in terms of proportional effect on the population, killing perhaps two million people, a third of Russian people.
- La Rinconada, the highest elevated city on earth has a gold mine where miners work for 30 days without pay. On the 31st day they are allowed to take as much ore as they can carry on their shoulders.
- In 2014 the world's largest cocaine producer is Peru. It has dethroned Colombia.
- The mysterious 120-ton boulder walls of an ancient fortress in Sacsayhuaman have survived thousands of years, including earthquakes, in part because they are "fit together with such precision you can't fit a piece of paper between them".
- Incas in Peru would purposely deform infant heads to stretch their skulls out permanently; the nobility would have significantly longer skulls than everyone else.
- Iquitos is the largest city in the world inaccessible by road. It's located deep in the Amazon rainforest and has over 400,000 people.

The Philippines

- In response to the United States buying the Philippines from Spain for $20 million, Andrew Carnegie personally offered $20 million to the Philippines so that the Filipino people could buy their independence back from the United States. They declined.
- Rodrigo Duterte, vice mayor of Davao City in Philippines, has been credited with transforming *the murder capital of the nation* to *the most peaceful city in Southeast Asia*, primarily through illegal death squads targeting criminals. He was dubbed The Punisher by Time Magazine.
- The country with the most favorable view of the US is the Philippines, as of July 2013.
- The Philippines is one of the deadliest places in the world for politicians, with over 1200 political assassinations in the last decade.
- The Philippines celebrates July 4 to commemorate that day in 1946 when it ceased to be a U.S. territory and the United States officially recognized Philippine independence.
- In 1993 Pepsi ran a contest in the Philippines in which it promised 1 million pesos, roughly $40,000, to the person who found the number 349 inside his bottle cap. Pepsi went on to mistakenly print 800,000 winning caps, leading to outrage and death threats to Pepsi executives.

- 40 million people simultaneously lost electricity in the Philippines, including the presidential palace, sparking fears of a possible coup, only to find out that the power grid was compromised by the cooling pipes of one power plant which sucked 50 dump trucks' worth of jellyfish.
- Repurposed old US Army Jeeps, called "Jeepneys", are the most popular form of public transportation in the Philippines.
- The flag of the Philippines is flown with the red on top during times of war and the blue on top in times of peace.
- 3 of the 9 largest malls in the world can be found in one street, SM Megamall, SM North EDSA and Mall of Asia are along EDSA, Metro Manila, Philippines.
- There is a popular pastry in the Philippines called 'Pan de Regla", which literally means "Menstrual Bread".

Poland

- During the German Invasion of Poland, 720 Poles defended their position against over 40.000 attacking Germans, stopping their advance for three days.
- The world's thinnest house is just 1.2 meters / 4 feet wide and it is set between two buildings in Warsaw, the home is 10 meters / 33 feet in depth and about 9 meters / 30 feet tall.
- There is an ancient old growth forest bordering Poland called Białowieża Forest. It resembles what most of Europe looked like before the 14th century. This story of conservation has been well documented over the last 500 years and is almost as rich as the ecosystem the forest supports.
- Vodka was originally invented in Poland, first produced in the 8th century.
- In Warsaw, People born in a public transport vehicle are entitled to free travel until they die.
- Jadwiga of Poland (d. 1399) was a female king. Polish law had no provision for a female ruler (queen regnant), but did not specify that kings had to be male.
- During WW2, Poland had an officially enlisted bear in its army that would give ammo to troops. Voytek was his name.
- Near Gryfino, a mysterious forest has 400 pine trees all with a 90 degree bend at the base of their trunks – all northward.
- The Polish Beer-Lovers Party won 360,000 votes in Poland's first free and fair election, in 1991, winning 16 seats in the lower house (Sejm).
- The first president of Poland, Gabriel Narutowicz, was assassinated was assassinated on 16 December 1922, five days after taking office, amidst a right-wing propaganda campaign accusing him of being "an atheist, a Freemason, and a Jew".

- Poland actually did use cavalry charges against the Germans in WWII, and despite popular belief, most of them were successful.
- There is a 32 km² desert in Poland and the Germans used it to train before deployment in Africa during WW2.
- Up to 20 million Polish people live outside Poland, which compared to 38 million population of Poland makes it quite a big diaspora.
- From 2006 to 2007, Poland's Prime Minister and President were a set of identical twins.

Portugal

- Rio de Janeiro was once capital of Portugal, making it the only European capital outside of Europe. This was due to the Napoleonic Wars; the capital was moved during thirteen years to avoid Napoleon capturing the Portuguese capital.
- There is an international zip line between Spain and Portugal. It connects Sanlucar de Guadiana, in Andalucia, Spain, to Alcoutim, in Algarve, Portugal.
- Portugal decriminalized prosecuting all drug users in 2001 but those same drugs are still listed as illegal because "Otherwise we would have gotten into trouble with the UN", and the number of addicts has been halved since then. Portugal managed to reduce drug related problems by making it a public health concern, rather than a criminal offense.
- Although prostitution is legal in Portugal, it is illegal for third parties to profit from it. Making brothels are illegal.
- The Alcobaça Monastery is a Monastery in Portugal that has a specially designed well in its kitchen where fish would swim into its canals and get trapped, giving the Monks fresh fish every day.
- In Portugal there is an ancient city submerged in water, but during dry spells the water levels go down and you can see it. It's called Vilarinho Da Furna.
- The United Kingdom and Portugal have the oldest alliance and peace treaty in the world that is still in force, with the earliest treaty dating back to the Anglo-Portuguese Treaty of 1373. The British used this 570 year old Treaty to lease a naval major base in WW2 from Portugal.
- In Portugal all residents are considered organ donors by default.
- Between 1910 and 1926 Portugal had 44 governments, 20 military takeovers, and 12 presidents.
- Portugal established a tax on storage devices, which basically make buyers, pay extra because of "possible copyright infringement usage".
- Portugal's National Animal is a rooster that supposedly came back to life to prove a man's innocence.
- In 1925 a Portuguese man orchestrated (from prison) one of the biggest counterfeiting operations of all time. He faked currency-printing contracts

and over 200,000 real (but unauthorized) notes were printed. The 'fake' banknotes that circulated were equivalent to 0.88% of the Portugal's GDP.

- On April 12, 2013, the Portuguese parliament approved unanimously an amendment to its nationality laws which would permit the descendants of Jews expelled from Portugal in the 16th century to become Portuguese citizens.
- The leader of the movement for Brazilian independence from Portugal was the son of the Portuguese king and later became the King of Portugal himself, making him the leader of both countries for a short time before eventually abdicating both thrones to his children.
- In the 17th century Catherine of Braganza from Portugal introduced the custom of drinking tea in Britain, a custom very popular among the Portuguese nobility.

Qatar

- In Qatar homosexual acts between adult females are legal whereas homosexual acts between adult males are illegal.
- Since the banning of child jockeys, camel racing in Qatar has exclusively used robot jockeys.
- Qatar's World Cup bid promised air conditioned stadiums that would reduce the temperature by 20 degrees Celsius, and would be solar powered.
- Pregnant women in Qatar who are unmarried cannot legally receive pre-natal care or a doctor while giving birth.
- Qatar has a male/female ratio of 3.46.
- Only 15% of Qatar's 1.8million population is actually Qatari citizens. The remaining 85% is largely made up of South East Asian Construction workers.
- One of the venues for the 2022 FIFA World Cup will be Lusail; a city that does not even exist yet.
- Qatar, an absolute monarchy, has the highest GDP per capita in the world at $102,700.
- In Qatar, foreign female workers who report a sexual assault can be charged with illicit relations.
- Households in Qatar get their water and electricity for free.
- Qatar's flag is the only national flag having a width more than twice its height.

Romania

- The crown of Romania is made from steel taken from a cannon captured during their war of independence from the Ottomans.
- Romania shipped 93.4 tons of gold to Russia in 1916 so that Russia would safe keep the Romanian Treasure in the Kremlin until the end of the First World War. As of 2014, they gave back only 33 kg of it.

- When Ceausescu made abortion and contraception illegal in Romania in 1967, he created a baby boom whose members eventually became those most likely responsible for his fall from power and execution in 1989.
- There is a cemetery in Romania famous for their vibrant and colorful tombstones that artfully depict scenes from the buried person's life, most often involving how they died. Each tombstone also has a poetic epitaph inscription.
- Donated Bibles were sent to Romania and subsequently pulped into toilet paper because there was a toilet paper shortage.
- Romania has 3rd highest internet connection speed and it's around four times cheaper than in the US.
- There is a fountain in Romania that is dyed red in hopes to raise awareness of Hemophilia.
- The heaviest building in the world is the "Palace of the Parliament" in Romania. For the construction of the Palace of the Parliament in Romania, over 9,000 buildings were demolished to make place for its construction, more than 1,000,000 cubic meters of marble and 3,500 tons of crystal were used.
- Vlad the Impaler is considered a national hero in Romania for keeping the Ottoman Empire from conquering Wallachia.
- Gypsies used to be hunted as a form of entertainment by some rulers in what is now Romania.

Russia

- During WWI, Romania decided to send its vast collection of treasure to Russia for safekeeping. In 1918, the new Soviet government cut all diplomatic ties and refused to return the treasure. Russia still holds the treasure valued at over $1.5 billion and has no intention of giving it back.
- Certain bears in Russia have become addicted to sniffing Jet Fuel out of discarded barrels. Going as far as stalking helicopters for the drops of fuel they leave behind.
- There are coffee houses in Russia where food and drink are free but you pay for time.
- Until 2011 in Russia anything under 10% alcohol was considered foodstuff and not alcoholic.
- In Russia many doctors "treat" alcoholism by surgically implanting a small capsule into their patients. The capsules react so severely with alcohol that once the patient touches a single drop, they instantly acquire an excruciating illness of similar intensity to acute heroin withdrawal.
- The purchase of Alaska from Russia by the U.S. was originally mocked by U.S. citizens, who called it "Andrew Johnson's polar bear garden".

- Around 1,311 people live in Verkhoyansk, Russia. A town with an avg. temp of -45 °C (-50 °F) in January, the city was attacked by a pack of 400 wolves last year. During part of the year the sun currently rises at 2pm and sets at 3:30pm.
- In 986, Vladimir the Great, audited the major religions before choosing one to unify Russia. Apparently he decided against adopting the Muslim faith because "Drinking is the joy of the Rus', we can't go without it".
- Chef Boyardee of canned Ravioli fame was awarded both the Gold Star order of excellence from the US War Dept. & the Order of Lenin from Russia for supplying rations to allied troops during WWII.
- Russia is suspected to have at least 15 secret cities. These "closed cities" are officially classified by the government, with their names and location unknown, they appear do not appear on maps, no road signs will direct you to them, and visits from foreigners are strictly prohibited.
- There's an American city 2.4 miles away from Russia.
- In Soviet Russia, prisoners would get tattoos of Lenin & Stalin, because guards weren't allowed to shoot at images of national leaders.
- In Yakutia, temperatures become so cold that trees explode, blue sparks fly from falling timber, mercury freezes and exhaled breath is transformed into a shower of ice crystals called "the whisper of the stars".
- On Russia's version of "Who Wants to Be a Millionaire" the audience misled the contestants so often they avoided the "asks the audience" lifeline.
- In 2010 a heat wave in Russia lead to the deaths of over 1,000 people, the majority of whom drowned as a result of swimming while they were drunk.
- Despite the famous Pearl Harbor event, Russia was the first target of a Japanese surprise attack. 37 years before Pearl Harbor, Japan launched a surprise attack on Russia, destroying much of the Russian fleet at Port Arthur. US officials applauded the attack for its ingenuity.
- In Russia, if you step on somebody's foot accidentally, you are expected to put your foot out so they can equally step on yours.
- The Tunguska Event, 106 years ago in 1908, was an unexplained explosion toppled some 80 million trees over an area of 830 square miles in central Russia. The energy of the explosion was estimated to be approximately a thousand times greater than the atomic bomb dropped on Hiroshima.
- At a depth of almost a mile, Lake Baikal in Russia is the deepest lake in the world. It is also the clearest and oldest lake while containing 20% of the world's fresh water.
- Russia is the biggest country in the world in territory. 17,098,242 square kilometers, counting for 13.9% of the world territory.

Rwanda

- The Parliament of Rwanda is the only governing body in the world where women outnumber men.
- Rwanda was the first country to ban plastic bags, they banned them in 2007.
- During the Rwandan Genocide, Muslims provided shelter and protection to both Tutsi and Hutu; this resulted in doubling the Muslim population.
- There is an area in Rwanda whose average monthly temperature fluctuates only two degrees Celsius throughout the year.
- Rwanda is a member of the British Commonwealth despite not having any historical ties with the British Empire.
- Once a month in Kigali Rwanda, everyone participates in a community service day known as "Umuganda," making the city cleaner.
- Young vagrants and petty criminals in Rwanda are exiled to an island where a youth "rehabilitation center" is located.
- Poor street children in Rwanda sniff glue to alleviate hunger pains.
- Rwanda has a solid tourism-based economy based on the mountain gorillas discovered by Diane Fossey.

St. Kitts & Nevis

- The United States and St. Kitts and Nevis are the only countries in the western hemisphere to have carried out the death penalty in the last 10 years.
- Saint Kitts was named "Liamuiga" by the Kalinago Indians who inhabited the island. This name, roughly translated, in English means "fertile land," a testimony to the island's rich volcanic soil and high productivity.
- Although small in size, and separated by only 2 miles (3 km) of water, the two islands were viewed and governed as different states until the late 19th century, when they were forcibly unified along with the island of Anguilla by the British. To this day relations are strained, with Nevis accusing Saint Kitts of neglecting its needs.

St. Lucia

- The small Caribbean country of St Lucia has more Nobel laureates per capita than any other country. 2 for a population of approximately 182,000.

St. Vincent & The Grenadines

- The country has no formal armed forces, although the Royal Saint Vincent and the Grenadines Police Force includes a Special Service Unit as well as a militia that has a supporting role on the island.
- In 2012 the main export was inflatable pleasure crafts.

Samoa

- On Samoa Air, passengers pay by weight, the more you weigh, the more you pay.
- In 1889 a German naval force invaded a village in Samoa, and by doing so destroyed American property. As American warships arrived in the harbor and prepared to fire on the Germans, a typhoon wrecked both the American and German ships. Both American and German navies failed to prepare against a devastating typhoon, because no nation wanted to admit to the other nation that they "were afraid of the elements".
- If you're a boy in Samoa you may be subject to the Fa'fafine, the Samoan tradition where a younger male child is raised as a girl.
- The time difference between Samoa and American Samoa, which are less than 100 miles apart, is 24 hours, after Samoa shifted westward across the international date line, to align its workdays with its Asian trading partners.
- Samoa completely skipped December 30th in 2011 in order to cross the dateline and go from being behind Greenwich to being ahead of it. They did this to improve trade with Australia and Asia, as it put them all on the same day of the week, rather than Samoa being a day behind.
- In Samoa, it's a crime to forget your own wife's birthday.
- In Samoa, homosexuals are accepted as a third gender.
- 93% of the population of Samoa neighbor, American Samoa, is overweight.

San Marino

- In 2013 the country of San Marino had only one prisoner. The crime rate in San Marino is so low that the San Marino prison only had one prisoner in it for almost a year. He was pampered with a private library, gym, TV room, and received his meals from a nearby restaurant.
- San Marino is the oldest surviving state and constitutional republic in the world, with its founding being dated as September 3, 301.
- University students at the International Academy of Sciences San Marino write their thesis' in two languages: both their native language and Esperanto, a constructed language. The goal is to remove any cultural or linguistic bias when presenting scientific content.
- People born in San Marino remain citizens their entire life and are able to participate in elections no matter where on earth they live.
- The tiny nation has a parliament that elects two people from opposing to share the role as Head of State for 6 month terms.
- There hasn't been a single fatality in Formula 1 racing since Ayrton Senna's fatal crash in San Marino in 1994.
- San Marino derives most of its income from the sale of postage stamps.
- The oldest constitution still in effect is the Constitution of San Marino.

Sao Tome & Principe

- From 2002 to 2009, Cocoa was responsible for more than an average of 50% of São Tomé & Príncipe exports.
- The islands of São Tomé and Príncipe were uninhabited before the arrival of the Portuguese sometime around 1470. Most of the earliest inhabitants were "undesirables" sent from Portugal, mostly Jews.
- By 1908, São Tomé had become the world's largest producer of cocoa.

Saudi Arabia

- In Saudi Arabia women are allowed to pilot aircraft, though they must be chauffeured to the airport because it's illegal for them to drive a car.
- There was a fire in Mecca in 2002 that killed 15 school girls. The girls were not allowed to leave the burning building by the state's religious police because they were not wearing correct Islamic dress.
- Saudi Arabia promotes practice of marriage between close relatives which has produced high level of several genetic disorder including thalassemia, sickle cell anemia, spinal muscular atrophy, deafness and muteness. 42% of marriages in Saudi Arabia are between first cousins.
- Saudi Arabia developed robotic camel jockeys because too many 4 years old slave boys were dying. Child slave jockeys were outlawed in 2005.
- Pokémon Trading Card Game for the Gameboy Color is banned in Saudi Arabia because "it promotes Zionism".
- Movie theaters have been banned in Saudi Arabia since the 1980s.
- In 2013 Russia out produced Saudi Arabia in Oil Production by 1,000,000 barrels per day.
- In 1979, the Grand Mosque in Saudi Arabia was attacked and taken over by Muslim terrorists. The Saudi government called a French counter-terrorism unit, but since non-Muslims are not allowed in Mecca, the French soldiers had to convert to Islam before they were allowed to liberate the mosque.
- In 2010 Pakistani diplomat Akbar Zeb was rejected in Saudi Arabia because his name can be translated to "Biggest Cock".
- To protect rights of Saudi women from evil of attractive men, Omar Borkan Al Gala, was deported from Saudi Arabia because he is too handsome.
- Saudi Arabia imports camels from Australia, and most of them wind up on a plate.
- The Flag of Saudi Arabia is never, under any circumstance, to be lowered to half-mast. As it bears the shahada, doing so would be considered blasphemous. It reads: "There is no god but God and Muhammad is the messenger of God".
- There are virtually no rivers or lakes in the entire country of Saudi Arabia.

- Saudi Arabia has a form of legal prostitution called a "sexual marriage". They write up a contract where the parties can be married, for example, an hour or two.
- Saudi Arabia produced, in 2012, 11,730,000 barrels of crude oil a day, the biggest producer in the world. Exporting almost 7 million of crude oil a day, being also the top exporter.

Senegal

- There is a lake in Senegal that is naturally bright pink. The French called it "Le Lac Rose".
- The most popular TV show in Senegal is a sheep beauty contest, Khar Bii, a reality television show consisting of a search for Senegal's most beautiful ram.
- The Wolof people of Senegal believe saliva contains blessings and knowledge, so elders welcome newborn children into the world with salivary secretion, the female elder spitting on the face and the male in the ear.
- The Africa Renaissance Monument in Senegal, which is meant to symbolize Africa rising up from oppression, was built at a cost of $27 million and was built by North Korean labor.
- In Senegal there is hugely popular wrestling sport that combines MMA style bouts with Sufi mysticism.
- All of Senegal's 92 deaths from participation in the First Gulf War were the result of an accidental 21 March 1991 crash of a Royal Saudi Air Force C-130H.

Serbia

- During the Serb-Bulgarian war in 1885, Serbia signed a one day armistice in order to allow Red Cross aid convoys to pass through Serbia into Bulgaria who had no medical corps. Serbia also donated some of their own supplies to Bulgaria.
- Serbia grows over one-third of the world raspberries.
- For mother's day in Serbia the Children "Sneak into their mum's room in the morning to tie her feet with ribbons so that she can't get up out of bed".
- During World War I Serbia lost 60% of its male population.
- A 100 dinar note from Serbia has Tesla on it.
- Despite the great distance, Japan and Serbia has excellent relations, the first signed diplomatic mission was on May 20, 1997 and both donated millions to each other in times of crisis. One of the most notable interactions between the two countries took place in 2003 when Japan donated 93 city buses to the city of Belgrade.

- As a condition of Serbia's acceptance of increased sovereignty for Kosovo, Kosovo's official name was changed to "Kosovo*", the first and only state in history to have an asterisk as part of its name.
- In 1989, 68% of pregnancies in what is now Serbia were aborted.
- Banatski Sokolac, a village in Serbia, erected the first Bob Marley statue in Europe as a symbol of tolerance in the Balkans.
- The urn containing Nikola Tesla's ashes is kept in the Museum in Belgrade.

Seychelles
- In 1981 a group of white African mercenaries tried to stage a coup d'état in the Seychelles, disguising themselves as a rugby and beer social club which donated toys to orphans. The toys didn't conceal the AK47s in their luggage well enough and the plot completely failed.
- In Seychelles, homosexual activity is illegal only for men, but not women.
- A Yorkshire man bought Moyenne Island in the Seychelles for £8,000 in 1962, and it is now the world's smallest national park and home to over 100 land tortoises.
- The Seychelles and Silhouette Island were named after Jean Moreau de Séchelles and Etienne de Silhouette, both ministers of finance under Louis XV, not seashells or silhouettes.
- The exports of Seychelles are around 75% fish.

Sierra Leone
- Sierra Leone has the lowest life expectancy in the world, with only 48 years average.
- There are people in Kenema that think Ebola is a hoax created by doctors to steal blood from patients, this made rioters trying to break down the hospital gates and rescue the patients inside.
- Freetown was once known as the "Athens of west Africa". In 1860, 22% of the colony was educated, compared to 13% in England. Education later declined and the current literacy rate is 40%.
- Sierra Leone is among the top ten diamond producing nations in the world and is also among the largest producers of titanium and bauxite; additionally it is a major producer of gold. Despite this natural wealth, over 70% of its people live in poverty.
- In 1992, a 25 year old army captain unintentionally overthrew Sierra Leone's president while trying to protest a shortage of boots and wages for his fellow soldiers, becoming the world's youngest head of state and ruling for 4 subsequent years.
- The lingua franca of Sierra Leone is the Krio Language; an English pidgin language derived from the Atlantic slave trade and brought to Sierra Leone

by freed/escaped slaves of Nova Scotia and Jamaica who immigrated to Sierra Leone in the late 18th/early 19th century.

- Ghana draws heritage and "slave tourism" with its luxury hotels, generally well-maintained historic sites and direct flights from the US, although historians argue that African-Americans are more likely to have roots in Sierra Leone than in Ghana.

Singapore

- Singapore has the world's highest percentage of millionaires, with one out of every six households having at least $1,000,000 US dollars in disposable wealth.
- Singapore bought billions of cubic feet of sand from Cambodia because Cambodia needs money and Singapore needs land.
- Despite its free-market image, all the land in Singapore is owned by the government, and 85 percent of housing is supplied by the government's own housing corporation. Basically, 22 percent of their GDP is produced by state-owned enterprises, including Singapore Airlines.
- Singapore is the only country in the history of the modern world to gain independence against its own will. On 7 August 1965, Prime Minister Tunku Abdul Rahman, seeing no alternative to avoid further bloodshed, advised the Parliament of Malaysia that it should vote to expel Singapore from Malaysia.
- There is a $500 fine in Singapore for not flushing the toilet in a public restroom, and the police do random checks.
- Singapore, with a fertility rate of 0.79, held a "National Night" in 2012, designed to encourage couples to "create a population spurt" by "letting their patriotism explode!"
- You need to bid for the right to own and drive a car in Singapore. The current rate in 2014 is roughly $80,000.
- In Singapore, if you are convicted of littering three times, you will have to clean the streets on Sundays with a bib on saying, "I am a litterer".
- It is illegal to pee in an elevator in Singapore, and some elevators have a Urine Detection Device which detects urine odors, sets off an alarm, and close the elevator doors until the police arrives.
- Singapore has increased the size of its country by 20% since independence by "land reclamation", the process of creating new land from the ocean.
- Chewing gum is banned in Singapore, unless it is prescribed by a doctor.
- Every Singaporean-registered vehicle leaving Singapore must have at least a three-quarter-full gas tank; this was decided to discourage Singaporeans from going over to Malaysia simply to buy cheaper gas.
- In Singapore any public gathering of 5 people or more is illegal without a permit.

- Due to Singapore's lack of natural resources, it buys raw water from Malaysia at a rate of 3 Malaysian cents (US$0.01) per thousand gallons.

Slovakia

- There is an Easter tradition in Slovakia that includes men chasing women in traditional dress, soaking them in water, and whipping them in the legs when caught.
- According to a 2009 amendment to the Slovak constitution, speaking Hungarian in Slovakia will cost you 5,000 euros.

Slovenia

- The cave with the deepest vertical drop at 603 m (1,978 ft.) is Vrtoglavica (Vertigo) in Slovenia.
- A 6500 year old dental filling made out of bee wax was found in Slovenia, making it the oldest proof of dentistry in the world.

Solomon Islands

- The Solomon Islands (NE of Australia) have an indigenous race with ebony skin and blonde hair.
- There is an abandoned cruise ship, the world discoverer, in a remote bay of the Solomon Islands.
- In 1943, the Solomon Island had a very special unexpected guest; John Kennedy was patrolling the Solomon Islands when his patrol boat was struck by a Japanese destroyer. He and his remaining crew had to swim 3 miles to the nearest island.
- A watermelon can cost $70 in The Solomon Islands.

Somalia

- There is a pirate 'stock exchange' in Somalia where locals can invest in pirate gangs planning hijacking missions.
- In Somalia 95% of females face genital mutilation, mostly between the ages of 4 and 11.
- Firms illegally dumped nuclear waste off Somalia coast, which was brought to the coast by a Tsunami, causing radiation sickness to the local villagers in 2005.
- There is an unrecognized state in Somalia called Somaliland which seems polar opposite with Somalia, with not only a functionally government and a safe state but also one of the better democracies in Africa.
- Somalia has a Minister of Tourism, even though there hasn't been an officially recognized tourist since 1990.
- The flag of Somalia was designed with the United Nation's blue color in honor of the UN's help in gaining Somalia's independence.

- Mogadishu, Somalia was rated as the #1 worst place to visit in the world.
- During the cold war Soviet Union switched from supplying aid to Somalia to supporting Ethiopia, backed by the United States. United States promptly switched their support to Somalia.
- A folk cure for mental illness in rural Somalia is being locked in a room with a hyena for 3 days.
- The city of Berbera is home to a runway designated as an emergency shuttle landing site by NASA.
- In 2011 Somalia's al-Shahab banned the popular snack samosa because triangular shape was not compatible with their strict version of Islam.

South Africa

- South Africa had, in 2013, the highest death rate in the world, 17 deaths for 1,000 population.
- When the world's largest diamond was discovered in South Africa, it was shipped to England on a steamboat under heavy security. However, it was a diversion, and the real stone was sent in a plain box via post.
- There was an American musician in Detroit, in the 1970s, who sold very few records in the US, so he quit music and became a demolition worker. In 1998, he found out that his records had gone platinum in South Africa.
- It is legal in South-Africa to equip your car with flame-throwers to prevent carjacking.
- South Africa has one of the largest impact craters on Earth. It is called the Vredefort Dome and is about 160 km in diameter.
- Pink Floyd's "Another Brick In The Wall" was banned in 1980 from South Africa because it had "become the anthem of a national strike of more than 10,000 "colored" (mixed) students and their white supporters".
- Table Mountain, Cape Town, South Africa is home to 2,200 species of plant, more than the entire United Kingdom.
- There is a fabricated shanty town in South Africa where tourists can pay to pretend to be poor.
- Just Nuisance, the only dog ever to be officially enlisted in the Royal Navy, earned a title and promotions, allowed to roam freely he used a train to get around the west coast of south Africa and was buried with full naval honors.
- South Africa generates two-thirds of Africa's electricity.

South Sudan

- South Sudan has the lowest literacy rate of the world. It is estimated that only 27% of the population over 15 can read and write. More specifically, 40% of the men and 16% of the women.

- The president of South Sudan wrote to more than 75 government officials and eight foreign governments in an attempt to recover $4 billion lost to corruption, promising amnesty and confidentiality.
- South Sudan does not have a single fully operational power station and everything has to run on diesel generators. To import each container, an entrepreneur must spend $9,500, fill out eleven documents, and spend sixty days waiting for approval from various offices.
- South Sudan's government plans to redesign its capitol city to look like a rhinoceros.
- Azania, Imatong Republic, Nile Republic, Republic of Kush, Republic of New Sudan, Wunjubacel, and Republic of South Sudan were some of the new names considered for independent South Sudan.
- In the few years since independence, South Sudan has started receiving foreign direct investment. The capital Juba has become one of the most expensive cities on Earth, and road building has started from the capital into the hinterlands for the first time.

Spain

- In 1492, the Catholic monarchs of Spain issued a decree banning all Jews from Spain. Sultan Bayezid, a Muslim, then sent the Ottoman navy to Spain to rescue the Jews from the Spanish persecution.
- Spain's Paralympic basketball team were ordered to return their gold medals won in Sydney in 2000 after nearly all of their players were found to have no disability.
- In 1625 English officers called off an invasion of Spain after their soldiers stopped off at a local winery and got hammered.
- There is a reason behind the name of the 1918 Spanish Flu. In the warring US, France, Germany, and Britain, censors suppressed word of the plague to maintain morale. However in neutral Spain, papers were allowed to report on it, giving the impression Spain was especially hard hit.
- There is a town in Spain where 700 people are descended from 17th century samurai who stayed there after an embassy returned to Japan. They have the surname "Japón", which was originally "Hasekura de Japón".
- In 1930 the US government barred and returned any mail from Spain bearing a new set of stamps, which showed a world-famous painting of a naked woman.
- There is a school in Spain that offers professional courses in prostitution, including positions, history, and laws concerning the trade.
- There is a museum in Spain where they have reconstructed two tyrannosaurus skeletons to show them having sex.

- The Caliphate of Cordoba, which was located in present-day Spain, under which Muslims, Jews, and Christians lived and worked together in relative peace and prosperity.
- Zookeepers in Spain installed a TV set in their chimp Gina's cage and then taught her to use a remote. While channel surfing, Gina discovered the porn station, to which she is now addicted.
- The Edificio Intempo is a 47-story building in Spain that was built, but they forgot an elevator.
- The small city of Almeria, Spain, which was dry and desert-like just 35 years ago, now produces more than half of all Europe's fruit and vegetables using imported soil, hydroponics and the largest collection of greenhouses on Earth.
- There are plans to build a bridge or a tunnel between Spain and Morocco, connecting Europe and Africa. It may have underwater tunnels for travel without interrupting ecosystems and ship travel.
- Spain sent 510 tons of gold to the Soviet Union for safeguard during the Civil War, and got none of it back.
- In 1680 King Charles II of Spain issued a decree stating that the Irish were to be treated as native Spaniards and were given all the same rights and privileges as a Spanish citizen due to the belief that the Irish were ethnically Spanish.
- The current King of Spain is believed to have shot and killed his younger brother Alfonso in 1956.

Sri Lanka

- It is the tradition in Sri Lanka for children to throw their baby teeth onto the roof of their house in the presence of a squirrel.
- There was a man from Sri Lanka that swallowed $670,000 worth of diamonds stored in condoms.
- Until approximately 600 years ago it used to be possible to walk from India to Sri Lanka. It is called the Adam's Bridge. The "Pumice" rocks float in water and support the theory that Indian King Rama's ape army built the bridge on water to attack the island of Sri Lanka.
- Sripada, also known as Adam's Peak, is a 2,243 meters (7,359 ft.) tall conical mountain located in central Sri Lanka, which is revered as a holy site by Buddhist, as the footprint of the Buddha, Hindu, that of Shiva, Muslim and Christian, that of Adam.
- Only 2% of the elephants in Sri Lanka grow tusks.
- Sri Lanka is the country with the most deaths from snake bites.
- The capital of Sri Lanka is Sri Jayewardenepura Kotte.
- Sri Lanka produces more than 90 percent genuine cinnamon in the world.

- In 1957, Sri Lanka attempted to get the Red Swastika implemented as a replacement symbol for the Red Cross in their countries, since the Swastika is a Hindi symbol of good luck.

Sudan

- Bir Tawil is a 2,060 km2 (800 sq. mi) area along the border between Egypt and Sudan, which is claimed by neither country.
- Sudan is the country with the most number of pyramids, with approximately 255 pyramids.
- Dinka tribesmen of Sudan sometimes rupture their stomachs by overeating in preparation for 'fat-man' contests. Deaths this way are considered an honorable way to die.
- In 2005, due to a typographical error while discussing the Sedan nuclear test site in Nevada, the nation of Sudan genuinely believed the United States was irradiating its citizens.
- The name Sudan comes from the Arabic term `Bilad -al- Sudan` which means "Land of Blacks".
- The Dinka people of Sudan take cow urine showers to turn their hair orange, a popular look for both children and adults.
- A man in Sudan was forced to marry a goat, because he had sex with it.
- Omdurman, the largest city in Sudan, has an average yearly temperature of 37.1 degrees Celsius / 99 Fahrenheit.

Suriname

- Paramaribo has the country's biggest mosque and synagogue sit side by side in the city center.
- Indians make up around 37% of the population in Suriname.
- The Dutch gave New York City area, New Amsterdam, to the English in exchange for Suriname.
- Suriname is bordering the European Union, due to the French territory of French Guyana.

Swaziland

- Sobhuza II was the king of Swaziland for 82 years and 9 months which is the longest documented monarchical reign. He had 70 wives, 210 children, and over 1000 grandchildren.
- As a consequence of HIV/AIDS that affects more than 25% of the population, life expectancy in Swaziland has fallen from 61 years in 2000 to 32 years in 2009.
- Swaziland's 1 Lilangeni coin is identical in weight and dimensions to the £1 coin and can be used in vending machines. It is worth £0.06.

- The country with the lowest life expectancy in the world is Swaziland, at 31.88 years, this is due to over half of adults in their 20s have HIV.
- Women are banned from wearing pants in Swaziland.
- King Mswati III of Swaziland banned sexual relations for Swazis less than 18 years of age for five years, he violated his decree after two months when he married his 13th wife, he was fined a cow.
- Flying broomsticks in Swaziland above 150 meters will be subject to arrest and a hefty fine.

Sweden

- Sweden pays high school students $187 per month to attend school, unless they miss classes.
- Sweden offers 480 days of paid maternity, and paternity, leave.
- The official twitter account of Sweden is given to a random citizen every week to manage.
- When you are in Sweden you have the year-round right to walk, cycle, ride, ski and camp on any land, with few exceptions, due to The Right of Public Access, or 'Allemansrätt'.
- Coca Cola sales in Sweden often drop more than 50% during Christmas, due to the tradition of drinking Julmust.
- While driving in Sweden, your car headlights have to be on at all times, even in broad daylight.
- Sweden is so good at recycling; it has run out of garbage and now must import garbage from Norway to fuel its energy programs.
- Ore trains in Sweden traveling down to the coast generate five times the amount of electricity they use, powering nearby towns and the return trip for other trains.
- The oldest living tree is a *Norway Spruce* in Sweden which is approximately 9,550 years old. This would make it around 3,000 years older than the invention of writing.
- In 1979, a number of people in Sweden called in sick with a case of being homosexual, in protest of homosexuality being classified as an illness.
- There is a city in Sweden using light therapy in bus stops to combat depression during winter, when 19 hours of the day are darkness.
- In Sweden BonusPappa is the word for Stepfather, they wanted to be positive.
- Swedish Navy detected underwater sounds suspected to be hostile Russian submarines in the 80s. The suspicion escalated to a diplomatic conflict between Sweden and Russia. It turned out later that these sounds came from fish farts, a discovery which led to the Ig Nobel Prize.
- Sweden has almost zero child fatalities in car crashes because most parents keep children rear facing until age 4.

Switzerland

- In Switzerland, Rabies has been virtually eradicated after scientists placed chicken heads laced with a vaccine in the Swiss Alps. The foxes of Switzerland, proven to be the main source of rabies in the country, ate the chicken heads and immunized themselves.

- Engineers building a bridge between Germany and Switzerland found that when the two halves met, their elevations differed by 54 cm. Germany bases sea level on the North Sea, and Switzerland by the Mediterranean; someone messed up the correction, doubling it instead of cancelling it out.

- The average teacher salary in Switzerland in 2010 was €90,000 / $112,000 per year.

- Switzerland has enough underground shelter to house the entire country's population and even more. This is due to a law that every house construction has to take in consideration a shelter for its inhabitants. Switzerland is the only country in the world that requires all of its citizens to have 24/7 access to a bunker.

- Switzerland has forbidden people from keeping lone guinea pigs because the animals are sociable and need each other's company.

- Men in Switzerland are required to keep the firearms they are issued during military service at home after they leave the military so as to prevent home break ins and have the countries men ready to mobilize in the event of a threat.

- There is a 500-year-old statue of a man eating a sack of babies in Bern, and nobody is sure why.

- Switzerland swore eternal neutrality in 1515 after losing the Battle of Marignano.

- In Switzerland if you fail your practical driver's license test 3 times you are required to consult an official psychologist to assess the reasons for your previous failures before you are allowed to retake the exam.

- Switzerland has no single Head of State, and instead has a seven-member executive council which serves as the Swiss collective head of state.

- One of Switzerland's main defense strategies is to demolish every main access into the country via roads, bridges, and railways. There were at least 3,000 locations currently prepared to blow at a moment's notice in case of attack.

- Scientology is considered a commercial enterprise in Switzerland.

- There is a bar in Switzerland designed by H.R. Giger, creator of the terrifying life forms and their otherworldly environment in the film classic Alien.

- Switzerland, often praised as a model for direct democracy, did not grant women the right to vote in all elections and cantons until 1990.

- Switzerland is abbreviated to 'CH' because of its Latin name, 'Confoederatio Helvetica'.

Syria

- Nowadays, the hamsters you see in pet stores are most likely descendants of two hamsters. In 1930 a zoologist went to Syria and brought back 11 newly discovered hamsters. Only 2 of them bred and their offspring were sent to laboratories around the world.
- Damascus, the capital of Syria, is the oldest continuously inhabited city in the world.
- Syria does not recognize its neighbor, Lebanon as an independent country, believing that it should be part of "Greater Syria".
- In Syria it was once a commonly held belief that using Yo-Yos would bring drought. As a result, they were banned country-wide in 1933.
- In 1958, Egypt and Syria joined into a single entity called the United Arab Republic. It lasted until 1961 when Syria seceded from the union.

Taiwan

- The Japanese occupied Taiwan with the intention of turning the island into a showpiece "model colony", contributing to development in Taiwan. As a result, the people of Taiwan in general feel much less antipathy towards the legacy of Japanese rule than other countries occupied by Japan.
- China banned the video game Football Manager because it treated Taiwan and Tibet as separate countries and was deemed "harmful to China's sovereignty and territorial integrity".
- It is customary for a death row inmate in Taiwan to tip his executioner from 500 to 1000 Taiwan dollars, about 20 - 40 USD.
- The Republic of China (Taiwan) claims land that is nowadays administrated by 10 countries including Mongolia, Japan, China, and Russia.
- Taiwan was under martial law from 1949 until 1987, the 2nd longest period of martial law in world history.
- The United States does not formally recognize Taiwan as a sovereign state. In fact, only 23 countries formally recognize Taiwan.
- In Taiwan, a signature has no value, but rather an official seal is used for authenticating a document.
- Taiwan has its own government, language, indigenous ethnicity and currency but is still considered to be part of China by most of the world.
- Taiwan paid $130M to establish diplomatic relations with Nauru, where it has the only embassy.
- In Taiwan it is not uncommon to hire erotic dancers to perform at a funeral.
- There is a Batman themed hotel room in Kaohsiung City.

- A significant portion of China's imperial treasures are housed in Taiwan's National Palace Museum.
- Taiwan has more than double of Reserves of Foreign Exchange and Gold than USA.
- Taipei, Taiwan, has free Wi-Fi for the entire city.

Tajikistan

- In the small Asian nation of Tajikistan, the unibrow is considered a highly attractive feature in women. If you are unfortunately born without a unibrow, you can paint it on daily to become more attractive.
- In 1911, a 7.4 magnitude earthquake triggered a massive landslide that blocked the flow of the Murghab River with 2 cubic km, .48 cu mi, of rock. It created a lake 56 km / 35 miles long by 3 km / 2 miles wide and is currently the tallest dam in the world at 566 meters / 1860 feet.
- 45% of Tajikistan's economy is from remittance, money sent by Tajiks in Russia back home.
- The tallest flagpole in the world, at 165 meters / 541 feet, is in Tajikistan.
- More Tajiks live in Afghanistan, and possibly Uzbekistan as well, than in Tajikistan, the land that takes their name.

Tanzania

- There are no current statistics on religion in Tanzania. Home to many faiths, its census hasn't asked about religion since 1967 in order to avoid a fight over which was the biggest.
- Albinos in Tanzania are at high risk of being murdered, hacked up, and sold in magic potions.
- The countries of Kenya, Tanzania, Uganda, Rwanda, and Burundi have plans to form the East African Federation by 2015. It would be the 11th most populated country in the world.
- Tanzania was formed when the countries of Zanzibar and Tanganyika merged in 1964.
- In 1962, a laughter epidemic struck Tanzania that caused people to burst into fits of uncontrolled fits of laughter, lasting from a few hours up to 16 days. Scientists are still unsure of what caused it.
- There is a lake in Tanzania with waters so caustic that it can burn the eyes and skin of animals who decide to go for a swim.
- There are over 120 ethnic groups in Tanzania, and the largest ethnic group is only about 14% of the entire population.
- The flag of Tanzania has the colors and symbols that carry cultural, political, and regional meanings. The green alludes to the natural vegetation and "rich agricultural resources" of the country, while black represents the Swahili people who are native to Tanzania.

Thailand

- In Thailand, police officers who are caught breaking minor laws are forced to wear Hello Kitty armbands for a few days.
- In 1880 the Queen of Thailand drowned while her subjects watched because they were forbidden to touch her.
- There are no common surnames in Thailand. Under Thai law, only one family can use any given surname, any two people of the same surname must be related.
- The children of the Moken people in Thailand and Burma are able to see clearly underwater due to their sea based culture.
- McDonald's serves spinach pies in Thailand.
- In Thailand there is a smile that specifically expresses "Yes, I know I owe you the money but I don't have it right now", and at least 12 others with specific meanings.
- Thailand's demand for edible insects is so high, they even have to import 800 tons per year.
- There is a Buddhist temple in Thailand constructed of an estimated 1.5 million beer bottles.
- A market in Thailand is run on top of train tracks. When a train comes, stall owners pack up their shops and move out of the way.
- There's a bakery in Thailand that makes bread that looks like human body parts.
- The full ceremonial name of Bangkok, Thailand is Krungthepmahanakhon Amonrattanakosin Mahintharayutthaya Mahadilokphop Noppharatratchathaniburirom Udomratchaniwetmahasathan Amonphimanawatansathit Sakkathattiyawitsanukamprasit. The longest in the world.
- It is illegal in Thailand to leave your house without underwear.

Togo

- The first shots in WWI are believed to have been fired in Togo, Africa. It was the German colony of Togoland.
- The national football team of Togo has an awfully unlucky streak and unbelievable history, including a helicopter crash, a bus ambush and murders, and a fake national team in the last six years. The former coach of the national soccer team of Togo created a fake team to play an international friendly against Bahrain.

Tonga

- In 1971, an eccentric millionaire tried to create a new country by hiring barges to dump sand on a reef in the Pacific. Tonga subsequently sent a military force to claim this new land.
- When a king dies in Tonga, the royal undertakers are not allowed to use their hands for 100 days afterwards. They are hand-fed in captivity, which is a step up from the older practice of having their hands chopped off.
- Captain Cook called Tonga the Friendly Islands because of his kind reception there, which was revealed decades later to be a deception for a failed ambush.
- 17% of all people from Tonga are Mormons.
- Tonga is the only Pacific island to have never been formally colonized.

Trinidad & Tobago

- In 1974 Trinidad & Tobago were denied 5 goals in a game they had to win to qualify for the World Cup. The referee responsible was then banned for life.
- It is illegal to wear camouflage clothing in Trinidad and Tobago.
- The largest ethnic group in Trinidad Tobago is of Indian descent.
- The Steelpan, steel drums used in Caribbean music, originated in Trinidad and Tobago.

Tunisia

- In Tunisia you can book an overnight stay in Luke Skywalker's boyhood home for only $10.
- All of the old buildings from Star Wars, such as Obi-Wan's house, Mos Espa, and Lars Homestead, are still intact and can be visited at Tunisia.
- George Lucas named the planet Tatooine after a village in Tunisia, Tataouine. He filmed scenes from the Star Wars in a place nearby. This name, Tataouine, is used in French to name a place far, far away.
- In 2010, Tunisia, a country that is 98% Muslim, has banned wearing headscarves in public.

Turkey

- Turkey has the biggest tea consumption per capita, with 7.5 kg in 2009, far away from the second place, 4.34 kg per person per year by Morocco.
- In Turkey, turkey is called Hindi, because they thought turkeys came from India.
- 1 sheep jumped off a cliff & 1500 sheep followed. Only about 400 died because the other sheep fell on a soft pile of wool/sheep.

- The term "genocide" was coined to describe the mass killing of the Armenians in modern day Turkey in 1915. An estimated 1-2 million were killed, wiping out much of the Armenian people's heritage and history.
- Speaking Kurdish in public was illegal in Turkey in the 90s.
- In 1876, the Sultan of Turkey gave marijuana to the United States as a gift. By 1880, Turkish smoking parlors were opened all over the northeastern U.S.
- In 1963 a man, after knocking down a wall while renovating his house, discovered an entrance to the entire Derinkuyu Underground City located in Turkey, it is supposed to have space for more than 20,000 people living in there.
- In Turkey boys aged 6 to 11 become a king for a day during their Sünnet Düğünü, a day of celebration for their circumcision that includes dressing like a king, eating sweets, receiving gifts, and partying with family, friends, and neighbors.
- İhsan Sıtkı Yener designed a Turkish keyboard layout after studies were made on letter frequencies and finger anatomy along with Turkish Language Association, which resulted in Turkey breaking countless world records in typewriting championships since its invention in 1955.
- Turkey had decriminalized homosexuality in 1858.
- Turkey has a morgue equipped with the latest in alarms and motion detectors in case any of the bodies stored there have been declared dead by mistake.
- There is an industry to sell seat belt buckles meant to trick a car's warning into thinking that you are buckled up.

Turkmenistan

- In Ashgabat, the capital city, water, gas and electricity are free.
- In Turkmenistan, car drivers are entitled to 120 Liters of free petrol a month.
- Former Turkmenistan dictator Saparmurat Niyazov banned lip-syncing, beards, gold teeth and circuses. He renamed months, food, schools and airports after himself and his family and made his book required reading for all. He even had a copy released into orbit so it could "conquer space".
- There is a "door to hell" that is constantly burning in Turkmenistan. It is the result of trying to burn a natural gas deposit and it has been burning for more than 40 years. The Soviet scientists planned to start a temporary fire to burn off methane in the area but didn't expect it would burn for several more decades.
- President Saparmurat Niyazov of Turkmenistan banned news reporters and anchors from wearing make-up on television, because he said he found it difficult to distinguish male anchors from female anchors.
- The capital of Turkmenistan has the highest concentration of white marble buildings in the world.

- Turkmenistan's ex-President Saparmurat Niyazov closed down all of the nation's hospitals that weren't in the capital city, his reasoning being that "the sick should come to the capital for treatment".
- The eccentric former president of Turkmenistan outlawed dogs because of their "unappealing odor", banned ballet, circus and opera for being "decidedly un-Turkmen like".
- The Flag of Turkmenistan is the most "Intricate" Design of All National Flags
- Turkmenistan president Niyazov ordered all ministers, members of parliament and civil servants to hike the entirety of a 37km 'Walk of Health' once per year. A path of stairs created by himself to improve national health.

Tuvalu

- One of the major sources of income for the small island nation of Tuvalu is the commercialization of the '.tv' top level domain. 10% of their revenue came from that. Idealab leased the right to use the .tv domain giving the island nation of Tuvalu enough money to join the United Nations in 2000.
- Tuvalu has no capital city but a capital atoll.
- The nation of Tuvalu's most valuable export is domain names.
- The official code for Funafuti International Airport in Tuvalu is FUN.

Uganda

- 50% of the population of Uganda is under the age of 15 and 75% of its population is under 30.
- Ugandan dictator Idi Amin full, sell-bestowed, title was "His Excellency, President for Life, Field Marshal Al Hadji Doctor Idi Amin Dada, VC, DSO, MC, Lord of All the Beasts of the Earth and Fishes of the Seas and Conqueror of the British Empire in Africa in General and Uganda in Particular".
- The people of Buganda, in Uganda, speak Luganda.
- Uganda's Minister for Ethics and Integrity once described raping schoolgirls as preferable to consensual gay relationships.
- Uganda has been among the rare HIV success stories primarily because of its openness. In the 1980s, more than 30% of Ugandan residents had HIV; this had fallen to 6.4% by the end of 2008, the most effective national response to AIDS of any African country.
- Uganda is the only tropical country to have participated at the Winter Paralympic Games, even though the athlete in question was living in exile in Norway.
- Indians were expelled from Uganda in 1972. President Idi Amin justified this action because of God told him to do it in a dream

Ukraine

- It is considered belittling and insulting to refer to Ukraine as "The" Ukraine.

- Porn is illegal in Ukraine, unless it is for medical use.
- Translated to English, the Ukraine's national anthem is "Ukraine Has Not Yet Died".
- In 1991 Ukraine inherited about 5,000 nuclear weapons when it became independent from the Soviet Union. By 1996, Ukraine had voluntarily disposed of all nuclear weapons within its territory, transferring them to Russia.
- The difference between "Ukraine" and "The Ukraine" is roughly whether it's a post or pre-Soviet context.
- Chernobyl continued generating power until almost 2001, due to an extensive power shortage in the Soviet Union and Ukraine.
- The name Ukraine comes from the Slavic word for "Borderland".
- Pripyat in Northern Ukraine has become densely populated with once endangered animals like the lynx and eagle owl after the city was evacuated, after the Chernobyl disaster. It is very interesting to see how the wildlife flourishes without any human involvement.
- 62.5% of Ukraine's population is Atheist or does not belong to any church.
- Ukraine is one of the world's largest exporters of corn.
- In 2001 China using a fake company tricked Ukraine into selling an ex-Soviet Aircraft carrier saying it wanted to make it a floating casino.

United Arab Emirates

- UAE has one of the highest ratio on male/female, with 219 men for 100 women.
- The religious authorities in the United Arab Emirates issued a fatwā against Pokémon because it encouraged gambling, and was based on the theory of evolution, "a Jewish-Darwinist theory, that conflicts with the truth about humans and with Islamic principles".
- In 2012, public sector workers in the United Arab Emirates got between a 35-100% pay increase, just because it was the country's 40th Anniversary.
- Only 9.5% of the United Arab Emirates' population is Arab.
- A city called Masdar City is currently being built in the United Arab Emirates; the city will only be powered by renewable energy resources with zero-carbon emission.
- According to the 2014 Social Progress Index, the country that treats its women with the most respect is the United Arab Emirates.
- In the United Arab Emirates, there is an ATM that dispenses gold bars.
- There's a beauty pageant for camels in the United Arab Emirates.
- You must have a liquor license to drink alcohol in United Arab Emirates.
- The largest car in the entire world is a monument built by the United Arab Emirates.

- 66.19% of the United Arab Emirates population is immigrants and 68.29% of that are Indians, making them around 44% of the total population.

United Kingdom

- Citizens of the Commonwealth, Canada, Australia and others, are allowed to vote in the United Kingdom.
- Since 1967 the United Kingdom Home Office only counts a homicide if the murder ends with a conviction making it nearly impossible to compare homicides rates between the UK and other developed countries.
- The United Kingdom is the only country that does not identify itself by name on postage stamps because the postage stamp was invented in the UK.
- The United Kingdom and Portugal have the oldest alliance and peace treaty in the world that is still in force, with the earliest treaty dating back to the Anglo-Portuguese Treaty of 1373.
- In the United Kingdom, Indian restaurants employ more people than steel making, mining and shipbuilding industries put together.
- In the United Kingdom, if a local or national election has resulted in a tie, the winner can be decided either by drawing straws/lots, coin flip, or drawing a high card in pack of cards.
- During the WWII, code breakers in the United Kingdom were recruited via a crossword puzzle contest in a newspaper. Successful participants were contacted and asked whether they would be prepared to undertake "a particular type of work as a contribution to the war effort".
- There are over 50 countries that celebrate a day of independence from the United Kingdom. Some of those countries were not independent until the 1980s.
- The United Kingdom has invaded, or mandated the invasion of, all but 22 countries in the world at some point during the last 306 years.
- Queen Victoria of the United Kingdom had an African goddaughter. Sara Forbes Bonetta was saved from becoming a human sacrifice by a captain in the Royal Navy who convinced her captors to make the young girl "a present from the King of the Blacks to the Queen of the Whites".
- The Union Jack, flag of the United Kingdom, is made up of the flags for England, Scotland and Northern Ireland. However the Welsh flag is not included. The Union Jack combines the red cross of St. George (England), the white saltire of St. Andrew (Scotland), and the red saltire of St. Patrick, to represent the three regions that make up the United Kingdom.
- The only person in the United Kingdom who is not required to have a driving license in order to drive is The Queen.
- There were a series of confrontations between Iceland and the United Kingdom 1958-1976 called the "Cod Wars".

- On March 28 1964, the first pirate radio station near England debuted, Radio Caroline. These pirate radio stations were created to circumvent the record companies' control of popular music broadcasting in the United Kingdom and the BBC's radio broadcasting monopoly.
- The shortest war in history was fought between the United Kingdom and the Zanzibar Sultanate and lasted only 40 minutes.
- The United Kingdom used 250,000 carrier pigeons for communication in WW II.

United States of America

- USA has more Olympic medals than any other country, 2,400 in Summer Olympics, and 16.3% of all medals given until 2014.
- The USA is the biggest producer and consumer of natural gas and refined oil products.
- The USA is the biggest importer of electricity in the world, importing almost 60,000,000,000 KWH, but that is not even 2% of their electrical consumption.
- The USA is the leader when it comes to the number of airports. There are over 13,000 airports, paved or unpaved, registered in the US, leaving the second place to Brazil, with only 4,093 airports.
- There are several big countries, but the US is the largest in railways, with 224,792 kilometers of railways. Enough for 5.6 trips around the world.
- The USA is the largest producer of corn, producing more than 50% of the world corn production.
- The USA is home of more than five million millionaires, more than any other country in the world.
- 60% of mid-size motels and hotels in the US are owned by those of Indian-origin, and of those, 1/3 have the last name 'Patel'. A name used by the educated-merchant class in Gujarat, India which means "landowner".
- After the American Revolution from the British, in 1777, Morocco was the first country to recognize the United States of America. The treaty is still in force, constituting the longest unbroken treaty in U.S. history.
- George Washington was the first head of state to be called "President", but back then the term was equivalent to "foreman" or "overseer". The senate objected because they didn't think he would be taken seriously with "a silly little title like President of the United States of America".
- In 1946, the United States of America tried to buy Greenland from the Danish for $100,000,000.
- There is a town in the United States of America that was inadvertently made uninhabitable by the spraying of dioxin, Agent Orange, at 2,000 times the level of the militarized version.
- The United States of America is not actually a democracy, but a republic.

- Harvard University was founded over 100 years before the United States of America.
- The Black Market in The United States of America accounted for 10% of its Gross Domestic Product in 2011.
- By the early 1890s, the private Pinkerton National Detective Agency employed more agents than there were members of the standing army of the USA.
- Due to the Second World War Restrictions in 1942, one could only purchase yellow American cheese in the United States of America.
- America had an Emperor; he was a homeless madman who declared himself "Emperor of these United States and Protector of Mexico" in 1859. He ate for free at expensive restaurants, declared war on Congress, and his funeral procession was 2 miles long.
- Contrary to other Nations the USA has no official language.
- In case of forfeiture, the seized property itself is considered the defendant, resulting in lawsuits with names like "United States of America v. $105,453.50, more or less, in U.S. Currency".
- The Wild Turkey was the bird Benjamin Franklin would have preferred over the Bald Eagle as the national bird of the United States of America.
- There is a town in the USA called "King of Prussia", and it houses the largest mall in America.
- In 1912, Japan sent the USA some Japanese Cherry Trees as a sign of their blossoming friendship. After WW2, Japan's Cherry Trees were weak and sick so the USA sent a bunch of them back to reinvigorate their trees.
- Until it was forcibly suppressed during WWI, German was the second most widely spoken language in the USA, with many local governments, schools, and newspapers operating in German.
- The 8th January 1836 is the last day in history that the USA had no national debt.
- When the slaves were freed from the USA, some went back to Africa and promptly enslaved the native Africans based on the plantation methods they learnt in the USA.
- You literally cannot be more than 107 miles from a McDonalds in the contiguous USA.
- Approximately 350 slices of pizza are consumed each second in USA.

Uruguay

- The President of Uruguay, José Mujica, donates 87% of his state salary and drives an aging Volkswagen Beetle. José Mujica was a member of the Tupamaros during the 1960s and 1970s, a group of urban guerrillas who robbed banks and businesses and distributed the money and food to the poor of Montevideo.

- Every county in the world is either entirely or partially north of Uruguay.
- It is completely legal to possess, grow, sell, and transport cannabis in Uruguay, the only country in the world to enjoy complete legalization. Uruguay's leading legalization activists don't support the new law legalizing weed, calling it "fascist" and a "step backwards" because the government intends to keep a database of users and impose limits on how much you can smoke.
- Uruguay is, by population, the smallest country to win a World Cup.
- The Uruguay national football team may be responsible for two deaths, two people committed suicide by jumping off a grandstand when Brazil lost the 1950 World Cup to Uruguay.
- In 1950 the Brazilian newspaper printed an early edition on the day of the final of the World Cup containing a picture of Brazil with the caption "These are the world champions". Uruguay's captain bought as many copies as he could and encouraged his teammates to urinate on them.
- There is a city on the Uruguay - Brazil border where they speak a mix of Portuguese and Spanish and there is no border control between the Brazilian side and the Uruguayan side. The language is spoken on the border between Uruguay and Brazil, and more specifically in the region of the twin cities of Rivera (Uruguay) and Santana do Livramento (Brazil). This section of the frontier is called *Frontera de la Paz* (Border of Peace).
- Uruguay is the top consumer of beef per capita in the world with around 61 kg/134 lb. a year.
- In 1865, Uruguay used hard cheese as cannon-balls in a war with Brazil.

Uzbekistan

- The oldest known chess set is over 1200 years old and was discovered in Samarkand.
- Uzbekistan is one of the two countries to be "doubly landlocked"; it is surrounded only by other landlocked countries.
- There's an island in Kazakhstan/Uzbekistan that was used as a test site and is now riddled with anthrax, smallpox, plague, etc.
- In 2002 the Uzbek regime boiled two political dissidents to death.
- Uzbekistan has the 4th largest gold deposits in the world.
- There is a statue of a large pineapple in Tashkent, dedicated to the successful cultivation of Pineapple plants, a venture that failed 4 months later.
- There are approximately 200,000 ethnic Koreans living in Uzbekistan, result of a deportation by the Soviet Union.

Vanuatu

- In Vanuatu, there is an underwater post office that has an underwater mailbox and a postman that will process your mail if you go to him.
- There is a cult in Vanuatu that worships John Frum, a WWII serviceman. Every year on February 15, they hold a parade to honor him, in the belief that he will return with wealth and prosperities, restoring the dropping of free cargo from planes, as in the war.
- During WW2 US military drove millions of dollars' worth of excess vehicles and equipment off the shore of Vanuatu, to make more room for returning troops.
- Prince Philip, Queen Elizabeth II's husband, is regarded as a god by some members of the Yaohnanan Tribe of Vanuatu. Their sect is called the "Prince Philip Movement".

Vatican City (Holy See)

- The Vatican purchased enough carbon offsets for the entire Papal city in 2007. To this day, the promised planting of a "Vatican forest" has not happened.
- When a journalist innocently asked Pope John XXIII, "Your Holiness, how many people work in the Vatican?" He replied, "About half of them".
- Vatican City is unable to join the European Union because the EU requires that all member states must be free market democracies.
- The Vatican City is home to the world's only ATM that gives instructions in Latin.
- The Vatican City has a crime rate of 133.6%.
- Vatican City has its own supermarket that sells wine and cigarettes tax free.
- The Vatican City is named after the hill that it's built upon; the name is dated before Christianity.
- Vatican City is only 0.17 sq. miles / 0.44 sq. kilometers. That means it has a Pope-ulation Density of 5.88 popes per square mile.
- There is a dress code for visiting the Vatican City, and vendors outside the entrance sell clothes made of paper to the unprepared.
- The obelisk located in the Vatican's Saint Peter square was originally brought from Egypt by Caligula himself.
- For a 59-year period ending in 1929, no Pope ever left the Vatican, a very tiny city.
- Vatican Bank is the main shareholder in 'Pietro Beretta' arms.
- The Vatican consumes more wine per capita than any other country.
- The police of Vatican are offered by Switzerland.

- From 1587 until 1983 there was an official "Devil's Advocate" in the Vatican whose job it was to play down the case for canonizing new saints in the Catholic Church.
- Vatican City has a 100% immigrant population.

Venezuela

- Since 2007, an unfinished skyscraper in Caracas has been re-appropriated by squatters into a vast 'vertical slum' which now includes grocery stores, hairdressers, and an unlicensed dentist.
- Venezuela owes foreign airlines over 4 billion dollars / more than €3 billion euros, leading many airlines to sharply reduce or stop service in the country.
- Gas prices in Venezuela are subsided and have been below $0.015 per Liter or $0.04 per gallon, depending on the exchange rate. Filling the tank of a Chevrolet Suburban can cost $1.54 compared to $120 in the US or $240 /€200 in some European countries.
- There is a persistent storm in Venezuela that produces lightning 140 to 160 nights a year, 10 hours per day and up to 280 times per hour, and it has been going since at least the 16th century. It is called Relámpago Del Catatumbo, or "the everlasting storm".
- Venezuela is one of the most violent places on earth with a person being murdered every 21 minutes.
- Venezuela has the largest proven oil reserve of any country in the world. However, it is only fifth among the OPEC in oil production.
- There is a small town in Venezuela, founded by German immigrants in 1843, that has maintained its authentic origin culture, including architecture, cuisine, and language, so much that it is known as 'The Germany of the Caribbean'.
- Venezuela is the top winner in the Big Four beauty pageants: Miss World, Miss Universe, Miss International, and Miss Earth, and was the second country after Brazil to win all four.
- Venezuela was the first country in the world to abolish the death penalty for all crimes, doing so by Constitution in 1863.
- In 2012 McDonald's in Venezuela charged the US equivalent of over $15 for a Big Mac.
- Venezuela is named after Venice, Italy. Explorer Amerigo Vespucci found a place where houses were all elevated from water as was done in Venice, and named it "Little Venice," or "Venezuela".
- Angel Falls in Venezuela is so high that the water often evaporates before it can land.

Vietnam

- Despite the infamous history of the Vietnam War, Vietnam today is one of the most pro-American countries in Asia, with 71% of Vietnamese people viewing the U.S. favorably in 2002.
- A gay Vietnam veteran has a gravestone that omits his own name, merely saying "Gay Vietnam Veteran," while pointing out that he received a medal for killing two men and a discharge for loving one.
- Approximately 40% of people in Vietnam have the surname Nguyen.
- The Vietnam War is known as "the American War" in Vietnam.
- It would take Vietnam an estimated 300 years and 10 Billion Dollars to clear its territory of unexploded bombs, shells and mines.
- The largest cave in the world is in Vietnam and has its own forests and clouds inside of it.
- Ho Chi Minh quoted the Declaration of Independence when he declared Vietnam's independence from France.
- In 1974, Vietnam attacked some Chinese troops stationed on a disputed island. In response, China destroyed the entire Vietnamese fleet and took control of the entire island chain.
- In Vietnam, it is possible to order a cobra blood wine from restaurant menus, the waiter will take a live cobra, kill it on the spot, drain the blood into a shot glass of rice wine, and top it off with the cobra's still beating heart for you to gulp down.
- Pirates stole internet cable and sold it as scrap causing most of Vietnam to get far slower internet access.
- In Vietnam, computer gaming is illegal between 10pm and 8am.

Yemen

- Due to its isolation, a third of the plant life on the island of Socotra is nowhere to be found on the planet. It has been described as "most alien-looking place on Earth". The Socotra Archipelago also 90% of reptiles and 95% of land snails that are found nowhere else in the world.
- Chewing of the drug Khat is so popular in Yemen that its cultivation accounts for 40% of the desert nation's water use. An average family from Yemen spends more on khat than food, an amphetamine like plant that more than 90% of Yemeni males are addicted to chewing.
- The coffee term "mocha" derives its name from the city of Mocha, Yemen.
- Shibam, the world's oldest skyscraper city, built in 16th century, is in Yemen and all its building are made of mud.
- When you lose your passport as a tourist in Yemen you have to place an ad in a newspaper for people to return it and wait three days before getting emergency papers in order to leave the country.

- In Yemen's internet cafes, you have to show your ID card before going on and then you're not allowed to hide your computer screen.
- Girls in Yemen can become married when they are only 8.
- Yemen's population is expected to reach 60 million by 2050 from 4.3 million in 1950, a 14-fold increase in just a century.

Zambia

- Coca-Cola's distribution network is being used to transport life-saving medicines to remote regions of Zambia.
- Zambia had a space program in the 1960s. It consisted of a grade school science teacher, a teenage girl and her cat, and a missionary. The plan was using a catapult launching system.
- Zambia's independence was declared on the day of the 1964 Olympics' closing ceremony, making it the first and only country to start the Olympics as one country and ending it as another.
- When the water is at a certain level in Zambia, an eddy forms at the top of Victoria Falls, allowing people to swim to the crest of the waterfall without going over. It's called the "Devil's Pool".
- President Kaunda of Zambia once threatened to resign if his fellow countrymen didn't stop drinking so much alcohol.
- Wysiwyg (What you see is what you get) is a name in Zambia.
- Benadryl is a prohibited drug in Zambia, and US citizens have been jailed and had their passports confiscated for mere possession.

Zimbabwe

- It is estimated that 70% of the population is unemployed, one of the highest in the world. Some sources even state the unemployment rate is 95%.
- The first President of Zimbabwe was called President Banana
- The people of an isolated tribe in Zimbabwe only have two toes, also known as the ostrich people, 1-in-4 people of the Doma tribe in Zimbabwe have only two toes on each foot.
- The dictator Robert Mugabe tried to stop a critic of Zimbabwe's hyperinflation by levying ridiculous taxes on his newspaper, the writer retaliated with advertisements printed on trillion-dollar-bills, which was cheaper than actual paper.
- Zimbabwe's bank balance was $217 at the start of 2013.
- In Zimbabwe, it is commonly believed that sex with an albinistic woman cures HIV. This has led to rapes and subsequent spread of HIV.
- There is a mid-rise shopping center in Zimbabwe which uses an air conditioning system inspired by African termite hills. It is ventilated and cooled by natural means, and uses less than 10% of the energy of a conventional building of its size.

- Harare is one of the most expensive cities due to its citizens switching to US Dollars as currency. They are so used to Zimbabwe money with very high values, that being charged $20 for a haircut seems a good deal as people do not have an outsider concept of the real value of the dollar.
- From 5 January 2007 to 14 November 2008 the inflation rate of the Zimbabwe Dollar was 89,700,000,000,000,000,000,000%, the highest inflation ever. To compensate they printed One Hundred Trillion Dollar-notes, which then was worth ~$30.
- An entire city in Zimbabwe was instructed to flush their toilets at the same time to unblock sewers.
- There is a 900 year old castle in Zimbabwe, Great Zimbabwe, which stretched nearly 800 hectares and was built in the 14th century; it served as a royal palace for the Kingdom of Zimbabwe. Artifacts within the ruined city suggest its inhabitants traded with merchants from Arabia and even China.
- In Harare one can purchase sadza nemunhu, a meal and a, prostitute, for US$6.00.

All this information was researched during the last months of 2014.

Printed in Great Britain
by Amazon.co.uk, Ltd.,
Marston Gate.